dream power

dream power

transform your life
through your dreams

Andy Baggott

A GODSFIELD BOOK

First published in Great Britain in 2000 by
GODSFIELD PRESS LTD.
A division of David and Charles Ltd.
Laurel House, Station Approach,
New Alresford, Hants SO24 9JH, UK

10 9 8 7 6 5 4 3 2 1

© 2000 Godsfield Press
Text © 2000 Andy Baggott

Designed for Godsfield Press by
The Bridgewater Book Company

Illustrations: Kim Glass, Ivan Hissey

Printed and bound in China

ISBN 1–84181–023-1

Picture Credits
AKG, London 10, 11T, 11B, 106 • Eric Lessing 48L;
The Bridgeman Art Library : Dreweatt Fine Art Auctioneers, Newbury, Berkshire, UK 14B
The Victoria & Albert Museum, London, UK 14T;
Corbis : Patrick Johns 66 • Joe McDonald 50R
Roger Wilmhurst, FLPA 55B • Jennie Woodcock 48R;
The Image Bank : Charles S. Allen 28 • M. Boada 47 • J.Carmichael 60T
David H.Hamilton 121 Romilly Lockyer 97 • Marc Loiseau 67 • Paul McCormick 51
Eric Meola 81, 122–123 • Michael Melford 52, 59 • Kaz Mori 109 • Steve Satushek 78
Joseph Van Os 20 • Hans Welder 24R;
The Stock Market : John Martin 25 • R.B.Studio 33;
Tony Stone Images 24L • Bruce Ayres 93 • Colin Barker 54 • Richard A.Cooke III 18
Andy Cox 124 • Tony Craddock 56 • Ken Fisher 111 • Bruce Hands 12L • David Hanover 113
Nancy Honey 98 • Rosanne Olsen 22 • Jeremy Samuel 32 • Philip & Karen Smith 34
Vera Storman 58 • Stuart Westmorland 60B

Special thanks go to
Francis Annette, Kate Barnham, Mark Barnham,
Tom Barnham, Wilf Barnham, Carla Carrington,
R. Hobbs, Kay Macmullan, and Eleanor Scott Plummer
for help with photography

Dedication
This book is dedicated to the memory and
dreams of Jacky Diaz (1963–99)

Contents

Introduction

This book will show you how to unlock the power of dreams so that you can gain a much deeper understanding of yourself. You will be able to use that knowledge to improve every aspect of your life.

The modern notion of dreams is that they are illusory or hallucinatory experiences that occur during sleep. This implies that they are unreal, and yet nearly everyone is able to describe a vivid dream from some point in his or her life that seemed especially real. Some dreams are so real that they linger on in the memory for many years, or sometimes even for a lifetime. Then there are stories of prophetic dreams – some of these dreams accurately describe future events in detail; others give the dreamer the answer to questions that have baffled him or her in "real" life. Wherever you go in the world, dreams appear in local folktales and mythology, and among some cultures they form an intrinsic part of people's spiritual practices and beliefs.

Our nighttime dreams can guide us toward a happier and more fulfilling waking life.

Perhaps modern science does not see the whole picture. Just because a person's dreams cannot be seen by others in the physical world does not mean that they are not real. We take it for granted that television, radio, and microwaves exist, yet we cannot see or feel them. Our ancestors regarded dreams as highly significant, and many tribal cultures still believe that the world of dreams is the real world and that the physical world is the world of illusion. Are they deluded, or are we?

This book seeks to show that dreams are real and tangible parts of our existence, whose power can be unlocked and harnessed. The first part deals with dreams and how to use, change, and understand them. The second part shows you how to interpret any dream, and from that interpretation, learn how to improve the quality of your life. The third part of the book shows you that it is your birthright to live in your dreams and create your own reality, if you choose to claim it.

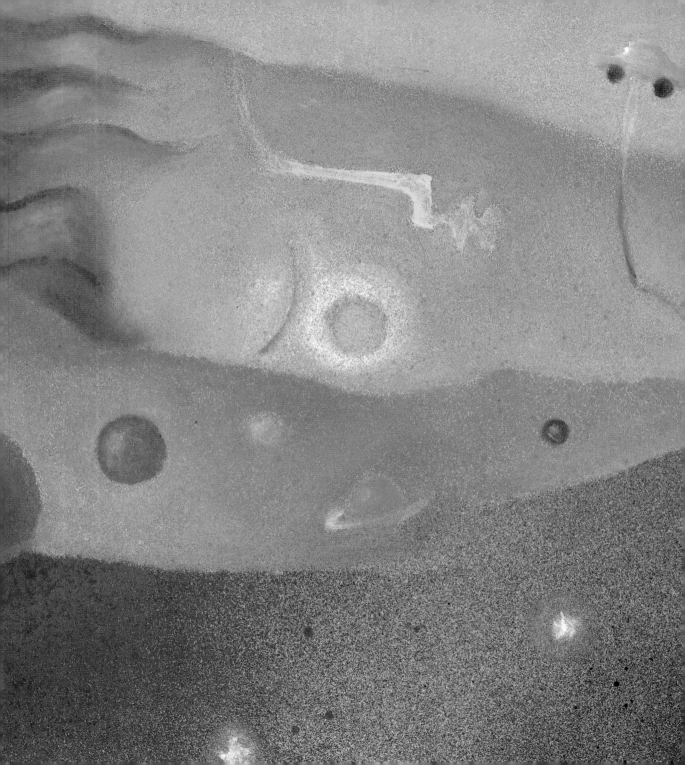

PART ONE *Walking in the land of dreams*

The land of dreams is a land beyond space and time. It is a realm where the impossible becomes possible, where fantasy and reality are one.

Dreaming is one of the most neglected areas of modern understanding. Many people think dreams are not real and should therefore be ignored. How wrong they are. We shall see that dreams provide a spiritual foundation for many people and can offer new insights and understandings that have a very real effect on the waking world we inhabit. We will discover the purpose of dreams and unlock the power to transform bad dreams into good ones.

To understand the true nature of dreams you must put aside all preconceptions and assumptions. This does not mean rejecting modern theories and scientific thought, merely accepting the possibility that modern society does not have the answers to everything. Theories are only collections of thoughts that best describe the facts, as we understand them. If you put those theories to one side and open your mind to the world of dreams you will encounter a realm of limitless possibilities — a multilayered land beyond the physical realm and therefore beyond the understanding of physical science.

Modern society thinks that we represent the pinnacle of creation and that our understanding of the universe is the most advanced that has ever existed on this planet. Yet the ancient Egyptians could build pyramids to a level of accuracy that lies beyond our current scientific and building skills. They could accurately predict the movements of planets and stars to a level that has become available to us only since the dawn of computers. On many levels they were more advanced than we are today. Their writings show that they clearly understood the significance of dreams, yet we reject such beliefs as "primitive." Perhaps we should think again.

The history of dreams

The ancient Greeks believed that dreams contained important messages from the gods and placed great store upon the prophetic power of dreams. In Homer's great epic, the Iliad, Agamemnon received guidance from Zeus's messenger in his dreams.

Since the dawn of time, all humankind has experienced dreams and, until modern times, has always placed great significance on them. Dreams are the one thing we have in common with everyone on Earth.

Throughout the ancient world dreams were regarded as communication from the gods. They were used to predict the future, to devise cures for ills, and to gain a deeper understanding of the physical and spiritual realms. More than three thousand years ago the ancient Egyptians produced writings about the interpretation of symbols in dreams, and prophetic dreams are mentioned throughout ancient Sumerian and Middle Eastern texts, including the Bible. The Greeks and Romans also placed great credence upon the prophetic aspect of dreaming. In the *Iliad*, Agamemnon is told in a dream by a messenger from the Greek god Zeus how to proceed in future matters.

An Indian text called the *Atharvaveda* dating from fifth century B.C.E. contains detailed descriptions of the interpretations of omens in dreams, while excavation of the ancient Babylonian city of Nineveh revealed a guide to interpreting dreams dating back to the time of the Babylonian emperor Ashurbanipal (668–627 B.C.E.). The most famous book of dream interpretation is Greek and dates from the second century C.E. It is called the *Oneirocritica* (from the Greek word *oneiros*, meaning "a dream") and was written by the soothsayer Artemidorus Dalsianus.

Throughout modern history, too, dreams have had a significant effect on many people's lives. The great French philosopher Étienne Bonnot de Condillac (1715–80) is said often to have brought to a conclusion in his dreams the reasonings on which he had been employed during the day. Benjamin Franklin (1706–90), the great American writer and politician, is said to have believed that he had often been instructed in his dreams how to resolve issues that preoccupied his mind. Samuel Taylor Coleridge (1772–1834), the celebrated English poet and philosopher, composed about 200–300 lines of his classic tragedy "Kubla Khan" while dreaming.

Dreams in art and literature

Dreams have been a favorite subject of artists through the ages. The aborigines have based much of their art on images derived from dreams and visions, as have the Native North Americans. In fact nearly all tribes throughout the world that include medicine men or shamans depict their dreams in works of art, because they regard the land of dreams as a powerful reality from which they can bring "medicine" (in the form of images and symbols) into this world.

Many artists from various disciplines have used dreams as their subject matter, including Pablo Picasso (*Dream and Lie of Franco* – etchings), Vittore Carpaccio (*Dream of Saint Ursula* – painting), William Shakespeare *(A Midsummer Night's Dream –* play), John Newman ("The Dream of Gerontius" – poem), and Edward Elgar (*The Dream of Gerontius* – music). Furthermore, many writers since the Middle Ages have used the narrative framework of a dream (called a dream allegory or dream vision). The most notable examples include Geoffrey Chaucer's *Book of the Duchess* (1369/70) and John Bunyan's *Pilgrim's Progress* (1678). As we can see, dreams have always been – and always will be – with us. For some people they have brought inspiration and insight. They have the potential to do the same for you.

Dreams have been the inspiration for many artists through the ages. This oil painting by Ingrès (1780–1867) is entitled Ossian's Dream.

From the Middle Ages onward, numerous writers have used dream allegories to convey messages in their works.

Dreams and healing

*I*n ancient Greece, dreaming and healing were very much interlinked. Sick people would take pilgrimages to oracular temples, where they would hope to experience healing dreams. At one time there were more than six hundred such temples dedicated to the Greek god of medicine, Asclepius, where individuals would offer sacrifices and perform rituals before sleeping in the temple in the hope that the god, or one of his messengers, would appear in their dreams to deliver a cure. This practice is also recorded in ancient Egyptian and Babylonian texts and is referred to as "dream incubation."

In ancient China, doctors would always interrogate their patients about the nature and content of their dreams as part of the initial examination. The *Yellow Emperor's Classic of Internal Medicine* (the founding textbook of Chinese medicine written around 2000 B.C.E.) makes comments on dreams and the nature of the pulse, which in Traditional Chinese Medicine form part of a deep and complex diagnostic technique (*see* right).

The nature of an individual's dreams can help a Chinese herbalist identify the source of a particular ailment. According to Traditional Chinese Medicine, unpleasant dreams can occur because of an imbalance of Yin or Yang.

YIN AND YANG

One must understand that ... the pulse consists of Yin and Yang. Thus one can know that when Yin is flourishing then bad dreams occur, as if one had to wade through great waters, which cause bad fears; when Yang is flourishing there occur dreams of great fires that burn and cauterize. When Yin and Yang are both flourishing there occur dreams in which both forces destroy and kill each other or wound each other. When the upper pulse flourishes then there are dreams as though one were flying; and when the lower pulse is flourishing there are dreams as though one were falling.

Dreams in African mythology

*T*hroughout Africa, dreams have always been important; they have even been known to change history. Different tribes have different ways of looking at dreams. Some regard them as journeys taken by the soul of the dreamer into the world of spirits. In this spirit world the dreamer might meet ancestors, saints, or other "guides," who could give the dreamer information or knowledge for him- or herself or others. Nightmares are regarded as the work of evil spirits or an omen of impending doom. Some people even claim to have seen these dark spirits, and

throughout Africa there are more than two hundred different names for malevolent dream-spirits. Two of the best-known ones are the Biloko, a dwarflike race that inhabits the rain forests of central Zaire, and the Tikoloshe, hairy monsters with the power to make themselves invisible or assume the form of human children.

In the central African republic of Burundi an elaborate belief system revolves around dreams. If a person has a nightmare, the dreamer can rinse out his or her mouth with a decoction of roots called *musendabazimu* ("spirit-chaser"). The herbal mix is then spat onto a fire accompanied by the words "I extinguish my dreams." Another belief is that if a person dreams of eating meat it means that a family member will soon die. The Hausa believe that when someone dreams, the soul roams free outside the body. If a Hausa dreams of falling, it means that a sorcerer (*maye*) is trying to catch the soul and the dreamer should return to the body. If a man has sexual dreams, it is seen as the work of a female *bori* (familiar spirit) having sex with him while he sleeps.

Some African tribes, such as the Hausa, believe that a person's soul wanders freely outside the body during the dream state. For this reason it is not recommended to wake someone suddenly, because it is a shock to the system when the soul is pulled quickly back into the body.

The Celtic fairyland

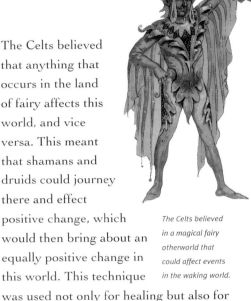

*P*erhaps one of the richest and most elaborate of dreamscapes is that of the Celtic fairyland. To the Celts, the world of dreams was as real as the world we inhabit. They believed that the two worlds existed in parallel and that, under certain special circumstances, one could travel between these worlds. Celtic mythology is filled with tales of fairy folk enchanting heroes into their land – sometimes never to be seen again or to reappear several hundred years later, having aged only a few days. In the land of fairy, everything is magical. Plants and animals have the ability to talk, either verbally or telepathically, and a host of mythical beings and creatures (including trolls, fairies, elves, dwarfs, ogres, dragons, and unicorns) inhabit this magical land.

The Celts believed that anything that occurs in the land of fairy affects this world, and vice versa. This meant that shamans and druids could journey there and effect positive change, which would then bring about an equally positive change in this world. This technique was used not only for healing but also for resolving disputes and divining the future. There were strict rules to be obeyed when walking in this Celtic otherworld, such as not eating any food or drinking any wine, since these were said to be enchanted with fairy magic and would prevent a return to the waking world.

Access to the fairy realm is said to be easiest at twilight, particularly on special days such as Halloween and Midsummer's Eve. Hills and sacred mounds are often said to conceal secret doorways, as are healing wells and other holy places.

Toilet of Titania by Richard Doyle (1824–83). Druids would "travel" to this parallel fairy world in their dreams to influence outcomes in the real world. Midsummer's Eve was considered one of the most sacred times to make contact with the fairy otherworld.

THE TALE OF OISIN

One misty summer's morning, Finn mac Cumhal, the captain of the Fianna of Erin, was out hunting with his son Oisin and many companions along the shores of Loch Lena. Suddenly, without warning, there appeared before them a beautiful maiden riding on a magnificent pure-white steed. Both the maiden and the horse were attired as royalty. The maiden wore a shining golden crown upon her head, and about her body she wore a dark brown mantle decorated with red and gold stars, which trailed almost to the ground. The horse wore silver shoes upon its hooves and a golden crest that waved gently as it trotted toward them.

As the maiden neared the group of hunters she said, "I have traveled long and hard from a distant land, but now my journey is at an end because I have found you Finn, son of Cumhal." And Finn replied to this, "Tell me of your land and your people, fair maiden, for your appearance is strange to me and tell me why you seek me."

"I am Niam of the Golden Hair," she replied, "daughter of the King of the Land of Youth, and I have come to you because of my love for your son Oisin." Then, turning to Oisin, she said in the voice of one who had never asked anything and been denied, "Wilt thou come with me to the Land of Youth, that I may share its beauty and my own with you?"

"I will follow you, my love, to the ends of the earth," replied Oisin to the maiden, for he was truly under a fairy spell, not caring for earthly things, but only for the love of this beautiful golden-haired maiden. So it came to pass that Oisin left the land of Erin with Niam of the Golden Hair and he was not seen again for three hundred years.

The Aboriginal Dreamtime

*M*ore than any other concept of the land of dreams, the Aboriginal Dreamtime is perhaps the most evocative and colorful, as is shown in their amazing artwork. Aboriginal art depicts the artist's understanding and relationship with the land of dreams, showing his or her "dreamings." This artwork uses traditional designs and symbols that can be "read" to tell the story of the dreaming.

The aborigines of Australia have a unique concept of dreams and their significance. Their mythology includes a belief in *Altjira* or *Altjiranga*, which can be translated as "the dreaming" or "dreamtime." Dreamtime refers to a time that has a beginning but no conceivable end. Dreamtime is another world or reality, from which the world as we know it was formed by mythological beings. These beings took the form of animals, plants, places, humans, or supernatural beings. Some held only one form whereas others were shapeshifters with the skill to assume many and varied forms. These beings were eternal, although some are no longer seen by humans or have metamorphosed into physiological features, such as hills, outcrops, and caves, which are now regarded as sacred.

Aborigines use music, song, and dance in order to achieve an altered state of consciousness as a means of entering dreamtime, so as to effect a change in that reality that will then filter down to the physical world. They regard dreamtime as the *real time*, and the world that we inhabit as merely the school of learning,

which we all attend. An aborigine will usually be accompanied on his or her journey to dreamtime by a power animal. This is a totemic animal that is of special significance to the individual and embodies positive attributes, such as strength, endurance, cunning, or objectivity, which help the individual to effect positive change in the land of dreams.

Dreamtime is at the core of the aboriginal belief system. Only the elders of the tribe have full knowledge of this world and therefore they have authority in all sacred and social matters. Dreamtime is celebrated in songs and ceremonies that form the *corroboree*, a social and ceremonial gathering. The aborigines are a nomadic people and, as they travel from place to place, they tell stories and perform ceremonies that celebrate the creation of that place or a significant battle in which the ancestors or supernatural beings took part in order to gain knowledge or wisdom. Their stories are passed down through the generations and not only form the basis of their belief system but also convey knowledge about the location of watering holes, places of safety or danger, sacred sites, and so on.

The aborigines enter dreamtime when they sleep and can also access it, when conscious, through ritual and music. They have no fear of nightmares because they understand that every dream comes to teach them and that it is through learning and understanding dreamtime that they can master all their fears.

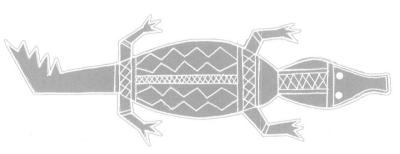

The Native North American dreamland

To the Native North American, the dream world is the real world. Around the age of 14 a Native North American boy is sent out into the wilds on a vision-quest to explore the dream world and seek a vision to enrich his life.

Many of the Native North American tribes (just like the aborigines) regard the land of dreams as the real world and the physical world as the realm of illusion. They believe that by seeking a vision in the land of dreams, they will find every truth that they seek.

When a Native North American boy comes of age, usually at about 14 years old, he leaves his tribe and enters the wilds with but one desire in his heart – to seek a vision. The vision-quest is a physical, emotional, and spiritual journey undertaken to empower individuals during times of change in their lives. The vision comes from "dreaming of animals in a lonely place" or from hearing "somebody sing" – perhaps a supernatural being in the guise of a moose or bear. These visions bestow supernatural animal powers upon the individual, and the animals in question act as personal totems, bestowing their own qualities upon the vision-seeker.

The vision-quest teaches people how to live with one foot in this world and one in the land of dreams. The Native North American land of dreams is a magical and beautiful place inhabited by supernatural entities and spirit helpers. It is believed that "everything has spirit" and that these spirits can be communicated with in the land of dreams. This means that animals, plants, and even stones can be spoken with and their wisdom learned.

Entering the land of dreams outside sleep requires a shift in consciousness. To help this shift, individuals seeking a vision will often fast for some or all of the ten or so days that they are out in the wilderness or forest. They may also deprive themselves of sleep to quieten the conscious mind and allow the subconscious mind to come to the fore. In the vision-quest they learn to face and master all doubts and fears. The truly important things in life – such as nourishing oneself physically, emotionally, and spiritually – gain importance in the mind, while the unimportant things – such as anger, pain, and grief – fade into insignificance.

ANIMAL TOTEMS AND THEIR MEANINGS

The following is a list of animal totems that are commonly seen during a vision-quest, together with their symbolic meanings:

BEAR	Strength, power, and determination
EAGLE	Clarity of thought and vision, objectivity
BEAVER	Industriousness, flexibility, and patience
DEER	Swiftness, eargerness, and gentle strength
ARMADILLO	Protection, endurance, and personal strength
BADGER	Tidiness, order, and organization
COUGAR	Independence and agility
MOUSE	Innocence and curiosity
RAVEN	Mystery and magic
MOOSE	Self-esteem and honor
BUFFALO	Prayer, sacredness, and abundance
COYOTE	Trickery and humor
WOLF	Loyalty and teaching
OWL	Deception and discernment

The processes of sleep and dreaming

The processes of sleep and dreaming have fascinated scientists and psychologists for years. Many and varied research projects have taken place, especially since the 1950s, to understand these processes.

The circadian rhythm

All creatures and plants on the Earth are sensitive to light, and many use this sensitivity to regulate changes in their metabolism. In larger animals this regulatory process involves periods of activity and periods of rest. One of the deepest and most rejuvenating natural relaxation processes is sleep. Some animals, such as bats and owls, sleep during the day and are active at night, but most mammals sleep at night and are active during the day. The adoption of a daily or circadian rhythm of sleep and waking is largely learned by a child from his or her parents, who in turn learned it from their parents and so on. It is neither natural nor unnatural to sleep at night. Our ancestors simply found that hunting and gathering were more successful during the hours of daylight, so they adopted the circadian pattern that most of us now use. Research has shown that humans can operate just as successfully at night, if they learn to change their circadian rhythm. What appears to be more important than when you sleep is the quality of sleep that you get.

Humans and animals function according to a circadian rhythm of sleeping and waking, the majority being active during the day and asleep at night. Creatures such as owls have an alternative circadian rhythm where they are active during the night.

Sleep and REM

As we fall asleep, a complex chain of biochemical changes takes place that alters our consciousness. During the night we alternate between deep levels of sleep and lighter levels, and it is during these lighter levels of sleep that dreaming takes place. Scientists know this because when someone is linked to an electroencephalogram

(EEG) machine to measure brain activity while that person experiences normal sleep, the most active time in the brain coincides with what is known as REM or rapid eye movement. It was noted that when people were in states of light sleep, their eyeballs darted back and forth rapidly behind the closed eyelids as if they were viewing some action or scene. Furthermore, if they were wakened during REM, they would invariably be able to remember their last dream clearly, even if they did not normally remember dreams.

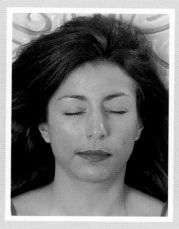

Dreams occur during light sleep – brain activity increases, and this results in rapid eye movement.

Dreaming

Most people have an average of five dreams per night. Often we are not aware that we are dreaming, so we rarely remember our dreams, but we certainly do dream. The number and the quality of the dreams that we have each night is largely dependent upon how long we need to sleep and how complex our biochemistry is. It is well known that certain foods, such as cheese, when consumed before retiring can cause nightmares. People who sleep for only two to four hours a night often have only one dream, but they manage to achieve deep sleep for a more sustained period of time than other people and therefore can survive quite happily on little sleep. George Ohsawa (1893–1966), the father of macrobiotics, slept for only two to three hours each night and led a very active life, writing numerous books and papers as well as touring and teaching all over the world. One of the main reasons for this was that he had a clear and untroubled mind. If your mind is clear, you require less rest, as we shall discover later in this book.

Why we dream

By adulthood the carefree dream world we inhabited as children has been pushed aside for mundane, day-to-day worries. Allow your mind to revisit the imaginative dream world of childhood because such dreams have the potential to guide you toward a more fulfilling life.

To the ancients, dreams were highly significant and important. They were an integral part of living on this planet and of gaining a deeper understanding of its many mysteries.

In our modern, "civilized" world we seem to have forgotten why we dream and why dreams are important on the path to happiness, health, and fulfillment. As young children we recognize that the world of dreams is just another reality with which we can interact. The child's world is full of dreams and imaginings, from fairies at the bottom of the garden to imaginary friends; children have an innate ability to let the mind run completely free. As we grow up, we are taught that all this "pretend stuff" is only for children and has no place in the "real" world of adulthood. So by the time we have grown up, most of us have abandoned our dreams and imaginings in favor of more commercial concerns.

We work in order to earn money to buy food and clothing and to provide shelter for ourselves. If that were the whole truth, life would be much happier for all of us, but it is not. We are taught that if we work harder and longer, then we can earn more money than we really need for these essentials, so that we can spend that money on "things" that will make us happier. In the vain search for such happiness we accumulate possessions and then spend more money trying to ensure that no one takes our happiness away from us. We pay for house security, insurance, and taxes for a police force in the hope that they will help to protect our happiness. How foolish we have become.

True happiness comes from within. If you abandon your dreams, you have no hope of finding it. Happiness is the stuff of which dreams are made. If you believe that dreams are an illusion, then you must believe that true happiness is also an illusion. Dreams are real; they exist and have energy. Earlier we discussed how occasionally we have a dream that really affects us, remaining in our minds long after we wake. Therefore, on some level, it must be real.

The dreams that you have when you are asleep and the dreams you can create when you are awake are one and the same – they are both signposts on the path to happiness, health, and fulfillment. The dreams you have when you are awake set your mind and energy on a path toward a goal. It is your right to seek the life of your dreams if you choose to. The dreams you have when you are asleep are messages and perspectives from other realities, which can help guide you toward the life of your dreams. The human mind is a wonderful piece of creation and has many levels and abilities that are untapped by modern human beings. The dream world, when understood, can empower and inspire you, teach and guide you onward and ever upward.

Everything is significant. The images and happenings in dreams are a language of metaphor and allegory. They can be read and understood in the same way as any language; and – once unlocked – this dream language can bring about wonderful insights, which have the potential to change your life forever. They even have the power to improve dramatically your physical, emotional, and spiritual health.

Every image or event in your dreams is significant. Once interpreted, they serve as signposts, directing you toward the life of your dreams.

How dreams can help us

Dreams can help us on many different levels, from simple problem-solving to understanding the deeper levels of our consciousness; from gaining inspiration and insight to learning how to feel happier, healthier, and more fulfilled.

Throughout history there have been instances when dreams have helped people. Some people have solved problems in their dreams; some have created music or poetry in them; others have experienced prophetic dreams that have saved their lives. Would it not be wonderful to have access to such resources on a night-by-night basis? Well, you can. Everyone and anyone can learn how to remember their dreams and interpret them.

Once you begin to open the door, you will discover a magical world that will teach you numerous things on many levels. This is because dreams are multidimensional. The world of dreams is beyond the limits of space and time. You can visit the past or the future in them, remain in this world, or journey to fantastic, mystical worlds – the universe is your oyster.

THE UNIVERSE AND YOU

If we compare you to the universe, what are you? You are a tiny speck among millions of tiny specks. You live on a minute dot of a planet in a minute part of the solar system, which makes up no more than a fraction of the universe. Compared to the universe, you are nothing. However, if we compare you to an atom or an electron, or even to a subatomic particle, then you are a whole universe within yourself. Everything that exists is a microcosm of the universe, so to understand the laws of the universe, you just have to understand yourself. Dreams and their interpretation can bring you that deeper comprehension of yourself and hence a deeper appreciation of the universe.

PROPHETIC DREAMS

Stories of prophetic dreams are too numerous to be dismissed merely as fables. Such dreams have been recorded since the dawn of the written word. From ancient Egyptian papyri and the Bible to the modern researches of scientists, there is a mountain of evidence to support their existence. H.F. Saltmarsh, a distinguished member of the Society for Psychical Research in the 1930s, recorded the following incident, which he investigated and concluded to be authentic. It concerned an upright citizen named John Williams and the 1933 Derby horserace in England. Williams was 80 years old at the time and for most of his life had been a Quaker and a staunch opponent of betting, drinking, and smoking. On the morning of the 1933 Derby, he woke from a most curious dream. He dreamed that he had been listening to the commentary of the Derby on the radio, which in itself was very peculiar because it was something he would never normally do. What was even more strange was that he heard the commentator call out the names of the first four horses. As he gradually woke he found that he could remember only the first two names, Hyperion and King Salmon. Later that day, but still well in advance of the race, Williams told two of his friends about his strange dream naming the two horses. When the race was being run, he listened to the commentary on the radio and heard the result – Hyperion coming in first and King Salmon second – just as he had dreamed it. The incident had such a profound effect upon him that he told all his friends and acquaintances about it, until it finally came to the attention of H.F. Saltmarsh, who recorded it.

Keeping a dream diary

Anyone can learn how to remember his or her dreams and how to keep a dream diary. This makes fascinating reading, even years after you have written it, and you can gain new insights and understandings about yourself each time you reread it. It is best to set aside a special book for your dream diary. You want one that is about 8¼ x 5¾ inches (21 x 15cm), so that it is easy to handle and write in while you are in bed. You also need a pen and, if you sleep next to another person, you may also want to have a flashlight beside your bed so that you do not disturb your partner during the night. You will find that once you have programmed yourself to remember your dreams, you will wake up several times each night, write down a few notes in your dream diary, and then go back to sleep again without losing any quality of sleep. In the morning you will wake feeling brighter and more refreshed than if you had slept solidly all night.

Keep a dream diary by your bed so that you can record your dreams immediately upon waking.

Remembering your dreams

Before you go to sleep each night, open your dream diary at a new page and write the date at the top. This sets an intent within your mind that you wish to record your dreams. Place your book, pen, and flashlight within easy reach. Before you go to sleep repeat the following five times:

"When I dream tonight, I will wake up at the end of each dream, write down my keywords, and go back into restful sleep. When I wake in the morning, I will feel rested and refreshed."

Then go to sleep. If you wake up with a dream in your mind, jot down a few keywords, then go back to sleep. In the morning, before getting out of bed, reread the entries in your dream diary. Allow the keywords to help you and write down all that you can remember about each dream. If any other memories come to you during the day, make a note and record them in your dream diary later on. Do not worry if at first you do not remember your dreams – have patience and persevere.

DREAM DIARY EXTRACTS

DREAM 1

KEYWORDS: **woodland path, house, chimney, snake**

I was walking along a woodland path and I saw a house with a snake protruding from the chimney. Later I found myself in the house and was aware that the snake was trying to slither down the chimney, but even though the fire was not lit, the chimney was hot lower down and the snake was not able to descend.

DREAM 2

KEYWORDS: **Watch repair, $15 (£9) replacement, small hands**

I had taken my digital watch to a jeweler to have the batteries renewed. The man applied a screwdriver to the watch, and suddenly both the watch and the screwdriver flew out of his hands and the watch was broken in pieces on the floor. The jeweler told me that I could have another watch to the value of $15 (£9), but all the watches were clockwork watches with small hands.

DREAM 3

KEYWORDS: **Old King Cole, garden fire, saucepan**

I was taking part in a concert and I was Old King Cole sitting on what looked like a pile of coal dust. I had to go to another part of the building for some reason and I passed some cars, and a policeman, who was dealing with a drunken driver. When I returned, I passed a garden bonfire and I could hear a noise like bubbling water. I got a garden fork and lifted the top of the smoldering grass and weeds, and I saw, underneath, a saucepan on its side and water pouring out of it like a waterfall, and there were steamed puddings cooking in the fire. Somebody said to me, "Well done!" then started discussing whether the pudding in the upset pan would be cooked or not.

Then somebody – a man, I think – took up all the puddings in his arms.

Bad dreams and how to deal with them

There is neither good nor bad in the world until human beings interact with energy. The way in which they interact determines whether that energy becomes a positive, constructive force or a negative, destructive one.

Some people are reluctant to delve into their personal dream world, either because they have sometimes had "bad" dreams or out of fear that they will experience something unpleasant. This does not necessarily mean having nightmares; bad dreams might, for instance, merely mean that the dreamer behaves in a way he or she perceives as bad. Whichever is the case, in truth there is no such thing as a bad dream – only the perception of one.

Anything in life that you think of as "bad" is only so because you perceive it as

"Bad" dream scenarios contain positive messages – being burned in a dream might teach you a greater respect for fire.

being bad, and the same is true of bad dreams. Even the most horrific nightmare is neither good nor bad until the person having it reacts to its energy. That is all everything is: energy. If you experience either a nightmare or a bad dream, you have a clear choice in how you react to that energy. If the experience teaches you something that makes you a wiser and better person, then it becomes a good thing. If, on the other hand, it causes you to become weaker and disempowered, then you have made it a bad thing.

A bad thing is a lesson unlearned. Everything that comes to us in life comes in order to teach us. If you can learn from everything, then the quality of your life will be forever improving. To be able to learn from everything requires total acceptance of all that comes into your life. Every time you fight situations, you give them attention and energy, thus compounding the problem. Once you learn to accept a situation, you can then learn from it, and as you do you will naturally draw energy away from it. Once you have learned everything that a situation has to teach you, it will cease to exist in your life. So if you experience bad dreams, learn what they are trying to teach you. In that way you will turn negative to positive, bad to good.

What's good and what's bad?

A child touches a hot surface and gets a nasty burn on his or her finger. Is this occurence a good or bad thing? If you focus your mind on the burn, on the pain and suffering that a burn gives a small child, then you will perceive it as a bad thing. If you understand that this relatively minor burn teaches the child a respect for fire that will save his or her life thousands of times over, then you will perceive it as a good thing. So does it actually count as a good or bad thing? This depends wholly upon how you

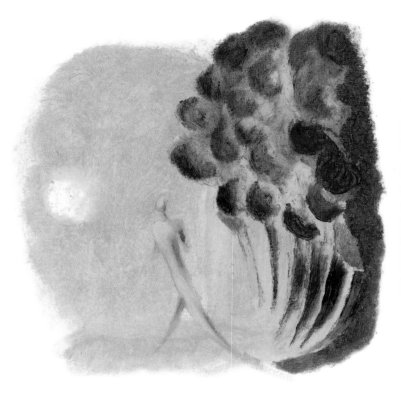

perceive it. If you perceive anything as bad in your life, seek to change the way you view it and you will, with perseverance, find a way of perceiving it as a positive thing. This is because there is neither good nor bad in the world until human beings interact with energy.

Remember that bad dreams are just another way in which your body tries to show you that something in your life needs changing to enable you to feel happier, healthier, and more fulfilled. Open your mind to perceive the dream in a positive way.

Changing dreams

The world of dreams is a world beyond the bounds of time and space. This means that dreams exist beyond these parameters, which in turn makes it possible to revisit a dream and replay the events exactly as they occurred the last time or to change things, if you wish.

Changing a dream is a bit like playing a computer game for a second time. You may visit the same or different rooms and you also know where to collect certain objects of power. You are also aware of rooms containing "enemies." If you learn to revisit a dream, the moment you make different choices, your dream will change and so will the outcome.

If you have a dream that you do not like, write down all the details. Then, put all thoughts of the dream out of your mind until you return to bed the following night. You can, if you like, imagine taking the dream out of your head and placing it under the pillow where it will be safe until the next night. Before you go to sleep again, reread the details of the dream three times. When you reenter the dream, you will find that you are almost

Dreams, both "good" and "bad," can be revisited in order to influence a more desirable outcome.

observing it from an outside perspective. You will no longer be closely involved and will therefore have the power, through thought, to change the outcome.

This technique, once mastered, can also be used to revisit positive dreams. You can review any dream from your dream diary and reenter it to learn more from it. If you cannot reenter your dreams while asleep, try the exercise to change dreams on waking as an alternative.

CHANGING DREAMS ON WAKING

If you wake up with an unpleasant dream in your mind, lie still
in the bed and mentally tell yourself not to wake up anymore.
This will allow you to maintain a semiawake level of consciousness
and you should then find it very easy to use your imagination
to reenter the dream and change it. The best thing to do is to
replay the dream three times in your mind. First, replay the dream
from your own perspective, observing the other things, people,
or animals that appear in the dream. If you are interacting with
other people, take special note of their mannerisms, body
language, and anything they say. Next, replay the dream from the
perspective of another participant of your dream. If you were alone
in the dream, replay it from the perspective of an ant sitting on
your head. Third, replay the dream from the perspective of a fly on
the wall. Observe it from an outside viewpoint. This will give you
a much greater understanding of your dream and then you may not
wish to change it anymore. However, if you do, revisit the dream
a final time and change whatever you wish into a more positive
outcome. All this will take only a couple of minutes and will allow
you to start the day in a much better frame of mind than if you had
simply got out of bed with the unpleasant dream still in your mind.

Dealing with nightmares

Recurring nightmares can be prevented by changing certain aspects of your waking life. Introduce simplicity into your life – keeping your bedroom clean and free from clutter will encourage a calmer mindset before sleep.

*N*ightmares can be both unpleasant and traumatic, but there are lots of things you can do to avert or change them.

The first thing to do is to look at your nutrition. Cheese, when consumed in the evening, has a reputation for causing nightmares in some people, but any food or drink eaten at the wrong time can evoke nightmares. Some nightmares occur as a result of a biochemical imbalance within the body and may be caused by a wide variety of foodstuffs, particularly foods and drinks containing artificial additives or sugar. Ensure that you do not go to bed hungry or feeling overfull.

If nightmares persist, the important thing to do is to initiate change, because this will alter both your perspective and your mental state before retiring. Change the routine you use, change your bedding and nightclothes, rearrange your bedroom, and fill your room with beautiful things such as plants, flowers, and crystals. If your bedroom is untidy, then tidy it up. A cluttered bedroom leads to cluttered dreams. You can also purchase or make a "dreamcatcher" and place it above your bed. It is said that if you place one above your bed, the dreamcatcher catches all the negative dreams and allows only positive ones to filter through and flow down the feathers into your mind.

You might also try to alter your perspective on bad dreams (*see* pages 28–29), or revisit and change them (*see* pages 30–31). If a demon or monster appears to you in a nightmare, why not try revisiting it and asking it what it wants to teach you? Embrace it, rather than fighting it.

CHILDREN AND NIGHTMARES

Children have wonderful imaginations and a natural ability to reenter dreams in their minds while awake. You can use these two factors to teach your child quite easily how to deal with nightmares. When your child is wide awake and in a happy frame of mind, play this game together. Get your child to imagine that he or she has a magic index finger – when the child points at anything and thinks the word "shrink," that object will shrink until the child says the word "stop." When the child is happy with this, get him or her to imagine being confronted by a big monster and using the magic finger to shrink it down to a size where it is no longer threatening. Now get the child to make friends with the monster. Ask questions about the monster's name, its favorite things, and so on. This will allow the child to view the monster in a fearless way. Once your child has learned to do this, you can teach him or her how to reenter dreams and nightmares and change the outcome, using the magic finger. Many children get so good at this technique that they gain the ability to do it in their sleep, the moment that anything negative appears in one of their dreams, so they never suffer from nightmares again.

Conquering fear and defying demons

To clear your mind before sleep, focus on a tranquil scene such as a beautiful, calm landscape.

One of the most important things to remember is that everything comes to teach us, and fear and demons are no exception. Once you learn to embrace them and recognize them as teachers, rather than as something "bad," your fears will subside and the demons will become your friends and allies.

If your life or your dreams are fearful and full of demons, you can free yourself of their hold upon you. Fear is neither a good nor a bad thing until you interact with it. If you fight fear or hold on to it, it will make your life miserable. But fear, although very real to the person who is experiencing it, is only a perspective. Things are only fearful because of the way you view them. A child learns that a monster appearing in dreams can be shrunk to a nonfearful size. All the child is doing is changing his or her perspective. And you can do the same.

Imagine that the world was going to end in two days' time. How much of what is in your mind now would still be there, if that scenario came true? All your fears and hurts from the past, or for the future, would cease to be of significance. Where you were going in your life would cease to be important. Family squabbles and unfulfilled desires would have no further relevance. You would learn to live in the "here and now." And it is by learning to live in the here and now that you can conquer your fear.

Are you in a fearful situation right now as you read these words? If the answer is no, then you have no need to fear in the here and now. All past and future fear is irrelevant. Learn to live in the present, and you will find that most of the time there is little to fear in life. The more you focus on negative thought-forms, the more likely you are to attract negative situations into your life. Spend your time making the very best of each moment, looking always for the lessons in everything, and you will enjoy a happy, healthy, and fulfilled life that is free from fear and demons.

Reprogramming your mind

Each night, just before you go to sleep, and each morning after you wake up, think a beautiful thought. Imagine something positive and happy that you have seen or experienced, or a scene of beauty and tranquillity. If you do this, you will naturally tend to see more of the beauty in both this world and the world of dreams. You create your own reality with your mind; you choose from which perspective you view life. There is beauty to be found in everything if you look for it. The well-known saying "beauty is in the

In the great scheme of things, family arguments are a waste of precious time and energy. Constantly dwelling on the negative is unproductive. Learn to live in the present for a happy and fulfilled life.

eye of the beholder" speaks the same truth.

Another truism is that "you reap what you sow." If you think negative thoughts, you will naturally see life from a negative angle, which will attract even more negativity into your life. If, on the other hand, you choose to think only positive, beautiful thoughts, letting go of all past anger and pain, you will have a quality of life beyond your dreams.

PART TWO *Interpreting dreams*

Anyone can learn to interpret his or her dreams. It just takes practice and
a little patience, along with a willingness to look honestly at oneself. Studying and
interpreting dreams can prove a deeply insightful and enthralling experience, which has the
potential to change your life for the better, forever.

Dreams can give us a multitude of information and knowledge, allowing us to gain access
to many different levels of perception. Whenever and wherever we walk, our minds are
constantly taking in impressions and knowledge. We all subconsciously study body
language, emotions, words, and a whole host of other stimuli. Dreams allow these
subconscious impressions to filter through to the conscious mind in order to help and instruct
us. Dreams will never tell you anything that, on some level, you did not already know. You
have within you all the knowledge and wisdom that you will ever need — you just do not have
access to it on a conscious level. Dreams allow you access to this inner wisdom, which will in
turn teach you a multitude of things about yourself and the universe around you.

The magic of dreams

Dreams give you information about things that your conscious mind has missed. Your mind
is a bit like a video camera that is forever rolling. If you go to a party where there are over a
hundred people, you might meet only twenty of them on a conscious level, but your mind will
have absorbed all of the people present. The woman at the bar, whose eyes you met for two
seconds as you were collecting your drinks transmitted a mass of information. In those two
seconds your mind will have taken an impression of every minute detail and placed it within
the memory banks of your subconscious. The man who bumped into you and stammered a
half apology will have initiated the same process. In fact, everything you see, feel, sense,
smell, taste, or touch is stored within the subconscious, ready to be accessed at the right time
in order to communicate something to the conscious mind. This is the magic of dreams.

How to analyze and understand your dreams

Symbols and themes in dreams contain messages for your waking life. Unraveling their meaning can help you to let go of negative emotions, such as anger and greed, and encourage a more positive outlook on life.

*T*here are simple ways to evaluate your dreams, and the more you work with them, the more you will understand their nature and meaning.

Look for the obvious

Whenever you are analyzing a dream, the first thing to look at is the obvious. Ask yourself, "Is this dream literally trying to tell me something?" Dreams can often give warnings or reminders. For instance, if you dream about having a flat tire on your car, the first thing to do is check your tire pressures. If you dream about something you had forgotten, the reminder will always be significant and you should think long and hard about its meaning, if it does not spring immediately to mind.

Look for metaphors and emotions

If the dream does not appear to have a literal meaning, look for metaphorical meanings, especially with regard to your personal feelings during the day or days prior to the dream. Try to see if your dream relates to recent events or things that have been preoccupying you. If it relates to long-past events, you need to ask yourself why these events are again coming to the forefront of your subconscious mind. Your dream may also be a signpost that you should become more in touch with your emotions. Ask yourself how you felt during the dream (e.g. happy, sad, fearful, strong). If you felt angry in a dream, you undoubtedly have some anger within you. The same is true of any "negative" emotions, which are emotions that weaken you. Negative emotions include anger, greed, selfishness, pride, and hatred.

Look for common themes and hidden meanings

You might also wish to make a note of general themes in your dreams, such as flying or falling. These often indicate a common experience or message although similar dreams may also have different significances and meanings. Be aware that dreams will not normally tell you something of which you are already consciously aware. If the dream appears to be dealing with something that you already know about, you need to look for another, deeper meaning within it.

Knowing a correctly interpreted dream

A dream is only fully interpreted when it makes perfect sense to the dreamer in the context of his or her present life, and evokes a positive change within the dreamer. If a dream leaves you feeling in any way dissatisfied, unmoved, or saddened, then you have not fully understood its message. Dreams always come to teach and empower the dreamer, never to confuse or weaken. If you feel confused by a dream, keep working on yourself and, as you increase your understanding, the confusion will lift. Out of chaos comes order.

Metaphors in dreams

The most common problem that people have in interpreting their dreams is understanding the meanings of metaphors. What does it mean when an animal, color, person, or object appears in a dream? The important thing is always to look at the dream objectively. Whatever image appears, look at its qualities and characteristics. Ask yourself whether it is hard or soft, living or inanimate, strong or weak, and so on. This will begin to help you understand what the image is trying to teach you.

Unlocking the language of dreams

*T*o understand the language of dreams, you need to understand how your mind and body communicate. Conscious communication through thought is but one of many communication systems maintained by the brain.

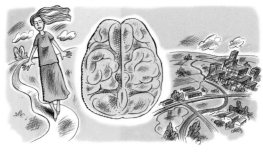

How the mind and body communicate

The mind and body communicate in metaphors or pictures. Once you understand the metaphor, you can appreciate what your mind and body are trying to communicate to you. Every dream you have is significant, although that significance is usually lost to us. We may wake up with the memory of a dream strong in our consciousness, but as we enter everyday living we get sidetracked and forget it. This is because the memories of dreams are stored in a different part of the brain from our normal consciousness.

The left side of the brain is the logical, conscious side. It draws in information and processes it; it is the area of the mind that learns and understands lessons. The right side is the intuitive side. It sees the big picture and perceives the path ahead, while the left brain finds the steps upon that path. The problem with many of us is that we have allowed the left brain to become dominant. Dreams are created and stored within the right brain, so by cutting off that side we cut off our access to understanding dreams.

The right brain allows us to think laterally, and this skill is essential in understanding the language of dreams, because in a dream a tree may not just be a tree. The left brain perceives only what it is shown by the right brain. If the right brain is shut off, the left brain can only perceive the physical world. However, when both left and right brain are working together, suddenly the left brain has many other worlds to perceive, including the emotional and spiritual realms.

EXERCISE TO HELP INTEGRATION
BETWEEN THE LEFT AND RIGHT BRAIN

The following exercise is designed to help you integrate
the two sides of your brain.

Find a quiet room, where you know that you will not be disturbed, and lie
or sit comfortably with your eyes closed. Say the following in your head,
"I want to communicate with my left brain." If your mind is full of thoughts
such as "Am I doing this correctly?" or "This is strange," then you are
listening to the chatter of your left brain. Ask it to be quiet, then tell it the
following: "You are a very important part of my being and I am grateful
that you have served me well thus far in my life. I would like you to
understand that you are not fulfilling your true potential, and I would
like to help you to become better, wiser, and stronger."
Next, say in your head, "I want to communicate with my right brain."
Then say to your right brain, "I thank you for guiding me thus far in my life
and I would like you to fulfill your true potential by becoming stronger
and an equal part of my consciousness."
Now visualize a strand of pure energy connecting your left and right brain.
Mentally introduce them to each other and tell them, "You are both vital
parts of my being. If you work together and cooperate, we can achieve
great things." Finally, bring your awareness back to the room, take a
couple of deep breaths, and open your eyes.

Colors and their meanings

*M*any dreams are in black and white; so when colors appear in dreams they are always significant. If something colored appears to you, even if it is just someone wearing a colored article of clothing, the color always has a deeper meaning.

The colors of the rainbow and their meanings

Red

Red is a very stimulating, dynamic color. We associate the color red with anger (as in "seeing red" or "showing a red rag to a bull"), but it can equally symbolize passion and desire – especially sexual desire. It is a warming, uplifting color and is used in healing to treat any illness where there is coldness or stiffness in the body. Red comes into our dreams to stimulate and inspire us. It is a sign that we need to create more movement in our lives.

Orange

Orange is another stimulating color but with a more gentle effect than the color red. It is associated with absorption of nutrients in the body – this means both absorption of nutrients from food and the mental absorption of knowledge from our experience. Orange comes into our dreams to tell us to think, think, and think again. It is a sign to let go of all that is "bad" and absorb all that is good.

Yellow

Yellow is the color of intellect and intelligence, the color of balance and harmony; it is used in color healing to treat mental disorders. It is also linked to the solar plexus of the body and to the function of digestion. Yellow comes into our dreams to tell us to seek balance in every area of our lives. It is a sign to watch our thoughts and actions.

Green

Green is the color of nature. It is linked to healing, harmony, and the heart. It is a neutral color of calm – neither stimulating nor suppressing; the most abundant color in all creation. It comes into our dreams to help us to heal. Green is a sign to let go of the past and embrace the present.

Blue

Blue is a cooling, calming color. It is associated with the ocean, and thus with the ebb and flow of emotions. It is used in color healing to treat ailments of the throat and has long been associated with truth. Blue comes into our dreams to show us truth. It is a sign both to speak and to walk truly day by day.

Indigo

Indigo is a calming, pacifying color that stimulates the right side of the brain and thus our creative and intuitive nature. It is also traditionally linked to the third eye, the psychic center of the body. Indigo comes into our dreams to show us hidden meanings. It is a sign to look at things from more than one perspective and may be a warning that all is not as it appears.

Violet

Violet or purple is the color of creativity, transformation, and spirituality: the color that connects us to our higher selves. This is the part of us that knows and understands everything; the part that is our connection to creation and to the divine. Purple comes into our dreams in order to connect us to our higher spiritual purpose. This color is a sign to look for the divine spark of creation within ourselves and let it shine forth.

Other colors and their meanings

Silver

Silver has always been associated with the moon and the powers of the goddess. Even in the Bible a silver cup is mentioned as a divinatory tool (Genesis 44:5). Silver comes into our dreams to show us a hidden message. This color is often a signpost that can lead toward the solution to unanswered questions.

Gold

Just as silver is linked to the energy of the moon, so gold is linked to the energy of the sun and the powers of the creator. Gold never tarnishes or rusts and does not deteriorate when buried. It, like the sun, is enduring and immortal. Gold comes into our dreams to give us inspiration and a spiritual message. It is a sign of high, spiritual insight and revelation.

Black

Black is a receptive color and is often symbolic of the Earth and death. In many cultures it is also regarded as a very protective color. Black stones were often used in magic as part of invisibility spells. Black comes into our dreams to warn and protect us. It may also be a sign that we need to let go of certain emotions or things that we are holding on to.

White

White is universally symbolic of purity and light. It too is a protective color and many people visualize surrounding themselves in a ball of white light before they go to sleep, to ensure a peaceful night's rest. White comes into our dreams in order to bring clarity. This color is always a positive sign, even if it appears in an otherwise "dark" dream.

Silver has long been associated with magic and divination – the color silver in your dreams conveys a hidden message.

Pink

Pink is the color of unconditional love. It has long been associated with peace, happiness, joy, and laughter. It comes into our dreams to lift the spirits and lighten the heart. It is a sign telling us not to judge anyone or anything, but to accept and embrace everything with love.

Brown

Brown is the color of the earth. It is associated with growth and "groundedness." It comes into our dreams to bring us down to earth. It helps us to connect to the earthly realm of plants and animals, and to access their wisdom.

Connecting with a color

If a color figures strongly in a dream, meditate upon that color and ask yourself how it makes you feel. Does it make you feel positive or negative? If you find the color in any way unpleasant, ask yourself what it is about the color that makes it so. It is always a signpost to some unresolved emotional issue within you. If the color makes you feel energized and positive,

Gold is connected with the powerful energy of the sun. This color appears in our dreams to give us spiritual insight.

you may wish to wear it or to place a piece of cloth of the same color by your bed or under your pillow at night. This will allow the color to teach and empower you through your sleep and dreams. Colors are powerful healers and teachers. They help us to find balance and harmony within our lives, if we choose not to ignore them. If a color appears to you repeatedly in a dream, this is almost certainly a sign that you need to make a stronger connection to that color in your waking life. Crystals and cloth are two of the best ways to carry a color with you. You need not worry about "listening" to it, or searching for the lessons that a color is trying to teach you – by wearing or carrying a colored cloth or stone with you, you will naturally attract the lessons you need into your life.

Animals in dreams

Animals in dreams provide an opportunity for great learning and understanding, if you are willing to listen to their wisdom. Even the most seemingly insignificant creature has its own wisdom to share. To discover an animal's significance you need to get to know the animal and understand the world from its perspective. Every animal has its own talents, and studying these can not only help you to understand its teaching but also to acquire those talents in your own life.

If an animal has appeared to you in a dream, look first at what the animal was doing. Was it behaving in the way it normally does in the waking world, or was it doing something unusual (e.g. talking to you)? It is also worth doing a bit of research about the animal, because this will give you a greater understanding of its character and teaching. Look at its habitat, its coloring, its nature, and the way it expresses itself (its song or call, the way it moves, its habits, etc.). All these things will increase your understanding.

Throughout the world, humankind has different relationships with animals. Some animals (such as the cow in India) are regarded as sacred, and many indigenous peoples regard all animals as sacred. This does not mean that these people are vegetarian; it means that they honor and respect every animal. To many Westerners, this idea is somewhat alien. In our world of intensive farming and overconsumption of meat we have forgotten how to respect animals. We see them as lower beings than us and, therefore, in some way less important. Many people have double standards: showering love on their pets, while eating meat that has come from animals kept in cramped, inhumane conditions. If we do not learn the true meaning of respect toward our animal allies, we will never really know how to respect ourselves.

Snake and lizard design from Ghana, West Africa. Discover the significance of two such animals in your dreams.

46

In dreams, even the tiniest creatures have much to teach us about ourselves and our destiny.

Understanding animals

The easiest way to understand animals is through observation and visualization. Choose an animal that you can easily observe (e.g. a pet, a garden bird, or an insect) and spend a few minutes studying it in action. Take special note of its movements, mannerisms, and any noises it makes. When you feel as though you have a broad understanding of how the animal expresses itself, find a quiet place where you will not be disturbed and imagine yourself as that animal.

Some people visualize themselves shapeshifting from their own form into that of the animal in their dreams. This allows you to experience fully what it is like to be that animal and to see the world from its perspective. Once you become adept at being animals that you know and can observe, you can then allow your imagination to take flight and assume any shape you like. You will be amazed at how much you can learn by this shapeshifting technique. It will also allow you to become any animal that might appear in your dreams, and so gain a greater understanding of its teaching. You may even like to try replaying your dreams that involved animals from the animal's perspective. You will be surprised at how different that dream becomes.

To understand fully the significance of an animal in your dreams, spend time observing its movements and habits to gain a true perspective of its world. You can then replay the dream and gain insights that you did not perceive the first time.

The symbolic meanings of animals

All animals have their own unique characteristics and talents. The following pages give you a starting point from which to begin to understand the meanings of an animal's appearance in your dreams.

Domestic animals

Cat

Cats have long been associated with mystery and magic, and were considered sacred by many cultures. They are at home in the dark and so make a wonderful ally in dreams, and they have always had an air of the spiritual about them. The Egyptian goddess Bast was depicted as a cat, while the Norse goddess Freyja has strong associations with this animal. If a cat appears to you in your dreams, everything about this animal is significant and should be noted – from its color and its eyes to its character and behavior.

Dog

Dogs are traditionally the companions of humans and highly protective of them. Each breed has its own characteristics, so if a dog appears in your dreams the first question to ask yourself is "What type of dog is it?" All breeds of dog share the characteristics of faithfulness and companionship, so they are usually a positive sign when they enter your dreams.

Rabbit

Rabbits have long been associated with fertility, and in Chinese astrology the sign

of the rabbit is associated with positivity and the moon. Perhaps the latter association is because it takes only one lunar cycle (28 days) for a baby rabbit to mature enough to be able to fend for itself. Rabbits also symbolize persistence and fleetness of foot.

Horse

There is so much myth and lore written about horses that it would take a whole volume to encompass them. The Celts held the horse as especially sacred, and the Welsh goddess Rhiannon was always depicted with a horse. Horses signify travel and freedom but have many other symbolic meanings, including sexuality and power.

Cow

In the West the cow has perhaps been one of the most cruelly exploited of all domesticated animals, yet it gives its milk and flesh to humans. The symbolic meaning of the cow is acceptance. If a cow appears in your dreams, look at those things you are finding hard to accept, and learn to embrace them with pleasure.

Goat

The meaning of the goat is steadfastness and flexibility. The goat is a very adaptable creature, at home on any terrain, and can eat a variety of foods. Goats make strong allies in dreams and will usually guide you on the path toward understanding.

Sheep

Sheep symbolize new beginnings. The lambing season announces the arrival of spring and with it new growth, so sheep in dreams usually bode something new. If a sheep is caught up in your dreams, it often means that something is stopping you from moving to new pastures.

Rodents

Rats, mice, hamsters, and gerbils are all intelligent and resourceful creatures, and most are highly sociable animals. They are also natural survivors, so they make good allies in dreams.

Rabbits symbolize fertility, persistence, and the ability to make a quick exit when needs must!

Wild animals

When a wild animal appears in a dream, its meaning is usually linked to its character and talents.

Alligator and crocodile

Both these creatures are noted for their ferocity and stealth. They are also excellent mothers carrying their newly hatched young to safe waters. This means that they have strong symbolic links to both life and death.

These magnificent long-necked creatures represent the ability to be objective and judge a situation from all angles.

Lion

The lion symbolizes strength, ferocity, and pride.

Armadillo

The armadillo is noted for its strong, protective shell, and so it has a symbolic meaning of personal protection.

Badger

This powerful animal has very strong jaws and feeds mainly on roots. It symbolizes strength, power, and "biting" through problems; it can also appear to help you get to the root of a problem.

Bat

This creature of the night symbolizes clarity of vision and facing up to the darker side of your inner self.

Bear

Some bears can reach speeds of up to 40 m.p.h. (65 k.p.h.) when chasing prey and can rip it to shreds in seconds with their powerful claws and teeth. The bear also

This nocturnal animal signifies clear-sightedness and is also associated with coming to terms with a darker side of your personality.

has the ability to store vast amounts of fat to sustain it through lean times. For this reason it has long been associated with strength, speed, and endurance.

Beaver
Known as the "master-builder" of the animal kingdom, the beaver is associated with constructing ideas and dreams, and with gaining power over unproductive emotions (water being always associated with the flow of emotions).

Giraffe
The giraffe, with its great height, is symbolic of objectivity or "seeing the big picture."

Deer
Deer are noted for their swiftness and alertness, and were especially sacred to the Celts. The antlers are sometimes regarded as psychic antennae, so the deer often appears as a warning of potential danger.

Bison (Buffalo)
The bison has long had strong links with humans. The Native North Americans would utilize every part of it: the meat for sustenance, the sinew for binding, the fat for cooking and sealing, the skin for warmth, and the bones for tools. The bison symbolizes help and sustenance.

Otter
This playful, fun-loving animal symbolizes the positive side of emotions.

The mighty bear is associated with strength, staying power, and swiftness.

Snakes regularly shed their skin, so dreaming of a snake is usually a metaphor for shaking off the past and making a fresh start. It is also symbolically linked to the cycle of death and rebirth.

Coyote

Traditionally known as "the trickster," the coyote is a powerful teacher, which shows resourcefulness and intelligence.

Donkey

Donkeys in dreams may help "carry" the dreamer through a process of change or spiritual progression.

Elephant

This majestic mammal really does have a long memory and is very loyal toward other elephants. It often appears in dreams to help you to remember something.

Snake

With its shedding skin, this reptile is linked to the powers of transformation and to ridding yourself of the past.

Fox

The cunning fox is noted for its ingenuity and is regarded by many cultures as a shapeshifter. If a fox appears in your dreams it is often a sign to look deeper into the dream's meaning.

Porcupine

The spiny porcupine is symbolic of gentleness and nonaggression, because it uses its quills as a means of protection only when its space is not respected.

Skunk

The skunk commands respect wherever it goes. It appears in dreams to teach respect of yourself and of all creation.

Squirrel

This rodent stores food for the winter, so it is linked to preparedness. A great climber, it can appear in dreams to help you achieve new heights of understanding.

Wolf

The wolf is noted for its keen senses and innate wildness. Many traditions have regarded it as sacred, with associations with the moon, good parenting, and guardianship of the land.

COMMUNICATING WITH ANIMALS

The normal conscious brainwave pattern of most animals is the same as our daydreaming pattern, so it follows that the best way to communicate with animals is to be in a daydream or meditative state.

Find a quiet place where you will not be disturbed, close your eyes and take a few deep breaths. Imagine yourself being transported to the natural habitat of the animal with which you wish to communicate, then spend a few minutes noticing the climate, vegetation, other animals, and so on. As you are doing this you notice the animal in question coming to meet you. Mentally welcome the animal, thanking it for appearing before you and telling it that you wish to learn from its wisdom.

You may ask the animal any question(s) you like. Open your mind to the answers that the animal will mentally convey to you. Some animals are highly communicative, whereas others are more reluctant to interact with humans. Be patient. It may take several attempts before you can strike up a dialogue with the animal. Once you feel that you have learned all you can, bring your awareness back to where you are sitting or lying. Take a few deep breaths, then open your eyes. Make a note of all your impressions, being aware that the answers to some of your questions may be cryptic or metaphorical. You can interpret these daydreams in exactly the same manner as you interpret a night dream (*see* pages 38–39).

Birds and their symbolism

Throughout history birds have been regarded as messengers or bringers of signs and omens. The ancient Romans employed a special soothsayer called an *augur*, who divined by observing the flight and cries of birds. The Druids did much the same and were especially fond of using the songs of birds such as the wren to predict the future. The practice of augury has largely been lost, although there are still a few shamans and medicine people who have the knowledge to practice this skill.

The symbolic meanings of birds

Bluebird
The bluebird is known as a bringer of happiness.

Crow
Crows are noted for their intelligence and ingenuity. They can easily outwit most other creatures and have the ability to adapt to a wide variety of environments.

Canary
The canary symbolizes finding your own voice and speaking your truth.

Rooster or cockerel
It takes only one cockerel to serve a whole brood of hens, so this bird has strong links to fertility. It is also noted for its dawn call, symbolizing alertness.

Chicken
Due to its relationship with humans, the chicken is symbolic of fertility and nourishment.

The proud rooster presides over a large brood of hens, hence its association with fertility.

Eagle

This magnificent bird of prey is linked to the energies of the sun. It symbolizes strength, endurance, and objectivity.

Dove

The dove's association with hope and peace goes back to biblical times. It is also noted as a good mother and so symbolizes nurturing and uplifting qualities.

Duck

Because of their affinity to water, ducks symbolize emotional balance. All ducks have the ability to dive and some can reach depths in excess of 100 feet (380 meters). A diving duck in your dreams means you have deep emotions to investigate.

Blackbird

The blackbird is a territorial bird and so is linked to protection.

Raven

There are many legends about ravens accompanying magicians, so they are linked to mystery and magic.

Crane

This bird has a long association with longevity and magic.

Goose

Geese symbolize protection. They mate for life, so are also linked to fidelity and loyalty.

Pigeon

The pigeon's strong homing qualities make it symbolic of protection of the home.

The majestic eagle with its mighty wings is symbolic of great strength, stamina, and objectivity.

The blackbird fervently guards its territory, so dreaming of this bird conveys the need for protection.

Magpie

This mysterious bird symbolizes all that is occult (unseen), both in this land and in the land of dreams.

Vulture

The vulture helps to recycle dead flesh, so it is linked to the cycle of death and rebirth.

Gull

The gull forms the boundary between the worlds of the earth and the sea. It is therefore regarded as a bird that bridges the worlds of sleeping and waking.

Mockingbird

This plain-looking bird symbolizes hidden or inner beauty.

Ostrich

This flightless bird embodies both groundedness and swiftness.

Owl

The silent hunter of the night, the owl symbolizes discernment and deception.

Peacock

This bird is linked to clarity of vision, because of its eyelike tail feathers.

Hawk

Hawks have excellent eyesight and appear in dreams to help you to see fine details that would normally escape your notice.

Swan

This noble bird is linked to purity, majesty, and wealth.

Stork

Traditionally the bearer of newborn babes, the stork symbolizes new beginnings.

In your dreams, the eyelike patterning on the tail feathers of the magnificent peacock symbolizes clear-sightedness.

UNDERSTANDING BIRDS

Many stories are told throughout the world of people who have the ability to change into the shape of a bird. Why not try it for yourself with the following meditation?

Imagine yourself being transported to a magical place where all things are possible. Once there, ask for the energy of a bird to visit you and feel yourself changing into that bird. Imagine your arms turning into wings, your feet becoming claws, and your mouth transformed into a beak. You will be amazed at how different the world is from a bird's perspective. Walk around in your imagination for a while and observe your surroundings.

Once you are familiar with your environment from the ground, you might like to try flying. Open up your wings and feel the air catch them as you gently lift off the ground. Notice the wind in your feathers as you soar higher and higher. Look down upon the world from this "bird's-eye" view. Make a mental note of all your feelings and impressions, because these will help you to understand the teaching of birds. When you feel that you have spent enough time as a bird, gently land; imagine yourself changing back into your normal shape and returning to this world. Next time you revisit a dream, perhaps you might like to revisit it in the form of a bird. It may help you to see your dream from a fresh perspective.

The water dwellers

*I*n both fresh- and seawater there is a
wonderful variety of creatures. Each has
its own place within a complex ecosystem,
where its talents are used to the full.

Deep-sea fish
All water dwellers tend to be linked to the
emotions, and deep-sea fish, such as cod,
haddock, and tuna, are symbolic of
connecting with deep emotions.

Dolphin
The dolphin is one of the most intelligent
of all creatures, with a natural affinity to
humans. It has strong links to healing and
protection, and there are many stories of
these creatures helping or healing people.

Eel
The eel symbolizes adaptability, flexibility,
and – due to its slipperiness – that which
is intangible or difficult to get hold of.

Octopus
The octopus, with its long tentacles,
represents seizing concepts that are
normally intangible to the conscious mind.
It is also regarded as a protective creature
because of its ability to squirt black "ink"
at its enemies as a defense mechanism.

Pike
This freshwater fish is noted for its ferocity,
so it makes a good protective ally in dreams.

Salmon
The salmon has long been associated with
wisdom. Celtic legend records the
salmon as being one of the oldest, and
therefore wisest, of all creatures, and in
the Celtic dream world this fish has
the ability to talk directly to humans,
offering insights and wisdom.

*The graceful seahorse acts
as a calming influence in
emotionally charged dreams.*

A whale in your dream encourages you to examine emotions buried deep within your consciousness.

Whale

A creature with the ability to swim to great depths, the whale is symbolic of searching the hidden depths of one's consciousness. It also embodies great strength and endurance.

Stingray

This creature symbolizes grace and respect: grace because of its beautiful, gliding movements; respect because of the sting in its tail.

Seahorse

This beautiful creature also symbolizes grace. It often appears in dreams to help transport dreamers smoothly through the realm of the emotions.

Seal

The Scottish call the seal the "selkie" and believe that is has the ability on certain nights to shed its skin and assume human form. There are many stories of selkie men and women charming humans with their beautiful singing. Seals are traditionally regarded as dream guides.

Trout

The art of trout tickling (using the hands to tickle and then grab it), when fully mastered, makes this freshwater fish easy to catch for food, so the trout embodies emotional nourishment.

Tropical fish

Most tropical fish are noted for their wonderful coloration, so they are often linked to color healing and inner calm. There is a great variety of types and colors, so if a tropical fish appears in your dreams its symbolism is often allied to the meaning of the color that it displays.

Turtle

The turtle has a long association with longevity and sacredness in many cultures. The Native North Americans call their land "Turtle Island." The turtle is able to move readily from land to sea, so it is also symbolic of making transitions from one state of consciousness to another.

The turtle is associated with long life and worshiped as a sacred animal. Its amphibious nature makes it symbolic of transition.

The symbology of insects

The caterpillar transforms itself into a beautiful butterfly. Dreaming of this insect shows you that you have the power to change your life for the better.

*I*nsects live highly ordered lives. They are always focused upon their tasks and never become sidetracked by aimless musings, as humans do. They are powerful metaphors in the land of dreams and have many lessons to teach us.

Ant

The ant symbolizes industriousness and tremendous strength. Each ant knows its own place within the community, so if an ant appears in your dreams it may be in order to help you find your place in life. Ants display none of the negative human traits of selfishness or greed. Each ant just goes about its work, seeking nothing in return except for sustenance. There is much to be learned from the appearance of these tiny creatures in your dreams.

Bee

Bees have the same sense of community as ants, but with the added bonus that they can produce honey. Bees appear in dreams to bring some sweetness to your life, and to teach you that you have the potential to be a king or queen if you truly learn to value yourself.

Butterfly

This insect is a harbinger of change. If a butterfly appears in your dreams it is often a sign that some kind of metamorphosis is occurring in your life and that you should embrace that change, for to resist it is to risk stagnation. The butterfly has the power to transform itself; it appears in your dreams to show you that you have the same power to bring about change.

Praying mantis

African mythology abounds in stories of the praying mantis. According to legend, whenever it got itself into trouble, it would go off and hide. It would then sleep and dream the solution to its problem. The praying mantis teaches lessons of introspection and stillness and should always be a welcome guest in your dreams.

A praying mantis teaches you to be still, take stock of your life, and reflect calmly on your problems.

THE TEACHINGS OF THE SPIDER

The spider is a brave and tenacious creature. It can build a web high in the rafters of a building; it can suspend itself from a tiny thread and swing in the air as it builds its web; and if its web is destroyed, it simply builds another. Anyone who has tried to clear spiders' webs from the home will know that, unless you remove the spiders as well, the webs always return within a day or two. The spider also has an eye for beauty. Have you ever seen an ugly spider's web? Once it has built its web the spider has to sit and wait for a fly to become caught in it, but the spider knows patience and will wait as long as it takes for the fly to come along. Most of the spiders that weave webs are female, which shows that patience comes more easily to women than to men. A seemingly insignificant creature, the spider can still teach us so many lessons. If a spider appears in your dreams, it is to teach all of the above and much more. The Native North American dreamcatcher (*see* pages 32–33) was originally created through observation of the spider, and this creature is perhaps one of the most powerful allies in the land of dreams.

A spider's appearance in a dream teaches us the virtue of perseverance. The Native American dreamcatcher was inspired by observations of a spider patiently weaving its web.

Mythical creatures and their meanings

Whenever a mythical creature appears in your dreams, it always has a deep, spiritual significance. These creatures appear so frequently throughout the legends of the world that they either have existed in the past or do exist now, but in another realm. Certainly they are much more than mere figments of the imagination. The best way to discover the meaning of a mythical creature, such as a dragon, unicorn, or thunderbird, is to read what has been written about it. Here is the story of the thunderbird, a mythical creature that is honored by the Native North Americans.

The story of the thunderbird

Long ago all humans, animals, and plants lived together in perfect harmony. There was no greed or avarice in the world, and everyone gave and took just what they needed to live, and no more. Each creature had its own particular talents and gifts that contributed to the overall harmony of the world. One creature though, the red hawk, could offer very little in terms of assistance to other creatures. All it possessed was its beauty and its wonderful song, and the red hawk traveled far and wide throughout the world displaying this beauty and singing its song.

Now in the western mountains lived a strange people called the thunder-beings. Their role was to act as gatekeepers. They kept the gates of the western winds and storms closed until the fall. When the fall came they opened the gates and sent the clouds across the sky, so that the land could be watered. When enough rain had fallen, they would call the clouds back again and close the gates until the next time. Red hawk used to visit the thunder-beings to sing its song to them and show its beauty, but it was one of only a few visitors, because the thunder-beings lived so far from the rest of creation.

It so happened that the thunder-beings began to complain about their isolation and became immersed in such misery that even the red hawk stopped visiting them. The next fall the gates did not open. The rains did not come, the grasses withered, and the lakes dried up. The animals, plants, and humans all began to die of starvation. They called out to the creator for help and, filled with compassion, the creator called red hawk to him and said, "Red hawk, I have seen the plight of the people and creatures because of the misery of the thunder-beings. I will give you a special gift to help."

The creator taught red hawk a special song and dance to be performed in a special way. So the red hawk flew off and gathered all the people together, telling them to build a special lodge. Red hawk entered the lodge and, once inside, began to sing its song and dance its dance. There was such power in the song and dance that the thunder-beings felt its vibrations in the distant mountains and were compelled by its power to open the gates and allow the rains to fall.

Later, the creator sent red hawk to serve the thunder-beings all the time. It became the thunderbird and is now the one who brings the storms. It flaps its wings to move the clouds back and forth, and the noise of this flapping can be heard as thunder. But you can never see the thunderbird, because lightning flashes from its eyes to blind us temporarily when it does appear. Anything that meets its gaze feels its power. The grass is set alight and the tree is split asunder, but we should always be thankful for the thunderbird, because without its work with the thunder-beings the land would be forever dry and barren.

The power and teaching of trees

Trees have been a source of symbolism since ancient times. Many have been associated with gods and goddesses, and are said to hold both healing and magic.

In Europe, dancing around the maypole has its roots in a sacred fertility rite.

Trees in mythology and custom

Different trees are associated with different traditions. Throughout Europe a birch or pine maypole is danced around every spring in honor of an ancient fertility rite. In the United States, the sun-dance is performed around a cottonwood tree, and sacred trees appear in nearly all ancient texts from every continent, including the Bible and Koran. In fact, nearly all religions, from paganism to Christianity, have symbolism attached to trees. The Celts held trees in especially high esteem as potent sources of symbolism and even had a tree alphabet. It is not only trees themselves, but the individual parts that make up a tree (such as the fruit, leaves, nuts, and bark) that are symbolic.

If trees figure in your dreams, the type of tree is of great significance, because each tree has its own characteristics in the same way that animals do. Here are some basic symbolic meanings of trees.

Bay

Sleeping under a bay tree is said to inspire prophetic dreams, as does placing its leaves under your pillow. It has traditionally been used to symbolize honor and victory.

Apple

Apples have long been associated with love and the goddess; in China they symbolize peace and harmony.

Ash

Odin, the Norse god, hung for nine days and nights from Yggdrasil, a mighty ash tree, in order to discover the Runes, so the ash symbolizes initiation.

Hawthorn

Used in magic for psychic protection, the hawthorn – with its white May flowers – symbolizes purity, chastity, and virginity.

Birch

To the Celts the birch symbolized purity, fertility, and cleansing and was the preferred wood for the Yule log that was traditionally burned at the winter solstice.

Bamboo

Generally considered lucky, bamboo represents flexibility and longevity.

Beech

This tree has been linked to the powers of wisdom, creativity, and divination.

Cedar

Native North Americans regard the cedar as a tree of purification. It is sometimes burned as incense or placed beneath a pillow to ward off bad dreams.

Coconut

Coconut is used in spells for chastity and protection, and is a symbol of fertility in India.

Elm

This tree symbolizes dignity, strength, and power.

Hazel

Used by the Celts for wand making and divining, the hazel is symbolic of truth and wisdom.

Holly

The "king of the winter," the holly embodies goodwill and joy.

Bay leaves symbolize honor and victory, and sleeping with bay leaves under your pillow may give you the power of prophecy.

Apples are a renowned symbol of love, and in China they are linked to peace and harmony of spirit.

Lemon

This tree represents sharpness of wit and purification.

Lime or linden

Used in herbal medicine as a calmative, it symbolizes feminine grace and beauty.

Oak

The oak abounds with symbolism. It stands for strength and endurance and is regarded as the summer counterpart of holly. It is also linked to wisdom, truth, fertility, and thunder. The acorn embodies the cosmic egg and immortality.

Eucalyptus

As well as being commonly used for treating colds and respiratory problems, eucalyptus is used in general healing spells.

Fig

Associated in some parts of the world with fertility, the fig is the cosmic or world tree in the Vedic tradition. The fruit of this tree represents truth, peace, and plenty.

Pear

The pear symbolizes hope and good fortune.

Pine

The pine symbolizes purity, uprightness, and enduring strength of character. It is also linked to longevity and immortality.

Pomegranate

This tree represents fruitfulness, plenty, and blessedness.

Walnut

The fruit of the walnut embodies hidden wisdom.

Willow

This tree stands for flexibility, adaptability, and emotional balance.

Yew

The evergreen yew symbolizes death, rebirth, and immortality.

CONNECTING WITH TREES

If a particular tree appears in your dreams, one of the best ways
to understand its meaning is to go out and find a tree of the same
variety and ask it to tell you its wisdom. This may sound a little
bizarre and far-fetched, but trees can actually have a profound
effect on your thinking, and just being physically next to a tree
can help you to unravel its symbolic meaning.

When you go up to a tree, ask it mentally if you can "connect" with
it. Provided your intuition does not say "No," make a physical
connection with the tree – either by touching it with your hands or
by sitting with your back against it. In the unlikely event that your
intuition tells you not to touch the tree, then find another tree and
try again. Once you have made a connection with the tree, close
your eyes and cast your mind back to the dream. Replay the dream
in your mind, then mentally ask the tree to help you understand it.
Now clear your mind and allow images to flow naturally into it.
Make a mental note of any striking impressions, and try to
remember as much detail as possible. When you feel ready, open
your eyes and note down all the images and thoughts that entered
your mind while you were connected to the tree. Compare them
with your dream and you may well find a new perception and
understanding that you did not have before.

Plants in dreams

When plants appear in dreams they can mean a variety of things. Note the stage of development of the plant – is it a seedling, fully grown, in bud or flower, or laden with fruit? Stages of development are often symbolic of the development of ideas or situations in our lives. Check whether the plant has any herbal or magical properties, because these may also be relevant. The more you research and understand about a plant, the easier its symbolism will be to read.

Basic symbolic meanings of some common plants

ALFALFA – protection against poverty

ALOE VERA – feminine beauty, intuition, and the moon

ANGELICA – the purifying power of fire and the sun

BALM (LEMON) – love and longevity

BASIL – love, strength, and courage

BAY – victory, wisdom, and purification

BELLADONNA – visions, dreams, and altered states of consciousness

BLACKBERRY – sacred to the triple goddess and the fairy folk

BORAGE – initiation, courage, and strength

CALENDULA (MARIGOLD) – the healing power of the sun

CAMOMILE – tranquillity, healing, and protection

CLOVER – luck and good fortune

CORNFLOWER – clairvoyance and psychic awareness

DAISY – love, light, and beauty

DANDELION – groundedness and vitality

EYEBRIGHT – clarity of thought and vision

FENNEL – courage and stamina

FERN – protection from thunder and lightning

FEVERFEW – calmness and objectivity

FORGET-ME-NOT – love and chastity

FOXGLOVE – protection and purity

GARLIC – healing and cleansing

GORSE – hope and positivity

HEATHER – humility, meekness, and good fortune

HONEYSUCKLE – the wisdom of the higher self

HOP – winter and the underworld

IRIS – purification and protection

IVY – tenacity and flexibility

JASMINE – meditation and psychic visions

LAVENDER – health and good luck

LILY OF THE VALLEY – hope and happiness

MARJORAM – mental clarity and longevity

MARSHMALLOW – love and protection
against dark forces

MEADOWSWEET – joy and lifted spirits

MINT – prosperity and health

NETTLE (STINGING) – protection against
lightning

PARSLEY – death and the underworld

PERIWINKLE – women's magic and
feminine intuition

POPPY – the land of dreams

PRIMROSE – growth and fertility

REED – truth and honesty

ROSE – universal love and acceptance

ROSEMARY – healing, righteousness,
and friendship

RUE – mental clarity and objectivity

SAFFRON – prophecy and sacred
knowledge

SAGE – purity, clarity, and truth

ST. JOHN'S WORT – peace and tranquillity

SNOWDROP – hope and consolation

STRAWBERRY – luck and love

SUNFLOWER – courage, action,
and the energy of the sun

TARRAGON – serpent energy and the earth

THISTLE – protection and independence

THYME – good health, good luck, and
sound sleep

VALERIAN – calmness and protection
against lightning

VIOLET – constancy in love

WOODRUFF – prosperity and modesty

YARROW – divination and clairvoyance

*Snowdrops in your
dreams represent hope
and consolation.*

69

Food in dreams

Dreams about particular foods can reflect certain desires – hot, spicy foods represent sexual appetite.

*I*n the West, our lives often revolve around food, so it is not surprising that food appears frequently in our dreams. Sometimes dreams can be dominated by food; on other occasions it is just one of many images appearing in your dream. In both cases it is significant.

Food can appear as an image in dreams for a variety of reasons. If it does, the first question to ask yourself is "Does the specific food have a unique meaning to me?" Is it a food you particularly like or dislike? First of all, look for the obvious. If the food has no special meaning to you, look at its color, texture, and the context in which it appeared to you. Was it hot or cold, fresh or stale, attractive or unattractive? How do you feel about the food?

Simplifying your diet by eating wholesome, additive-free food will help you to streamline your life and your thinking.

All images in dreams are signposts to your inner self, so the more questions you ask about the content and context of your dream, the more you will be questioning yourself. It is worth noting also the biochemical effect that different foods can have upon the body. Red meat, for instance, takes between two and four days to digest and, when eaten in excess, can produce emotions such as greed and anger. Sugar, tea, coffee, and alcohol are all stimulants that can produce extremes of emotions, such as elation or depression.

The body only speaks a natural language, so synthetic food and chemical additives tend to confuse the biochemistry, as does medication. Food is also linked to our desires; spicy or tangy foods that stimulate the secretion of saliva also

tend to stimulate the sex drive. Food is the single biggest factor in our health and well-being. You are what you eat, and when food appears in your dreams you should always check whether you are nourishing yourself correctly. A balanced diet of organic wholefoods and fresh vegetables will always produce dreams that are much simpler to understand than those produced by a diet of junk foods and stimulants.

Having a healthy relationship with food

Having a healthy relationship with food means much more than just eating a balanced diet. It involves your attitudes toward food and how you use it. If you use food to make yourself happy, then you are relying on something outside yourself for your happiness, rather than finding it within and for yourself. A dependent happiness such as this is a fragile, vulnerable happiness.

The most common problems with food relate to addictions. These occur when people have become so reliant upon a substance to make them feel better that they can no longer live without it. This is ultimately the path toward permanent sadness. If you are addicted to food, or use it to make you feel happy, the following rules will help you to find freedom from dependence on food.

If you are unhappy, change your thinking from negative to positive, first using the power of your own mind, and then reward yourself with your favorite food. Never cook or eat when you are stressed or in a bad mood, because you will just be consuming more stress.

When you are not happy, eat simply. Only when you are happy can you safely eat a wider diet.

For optimum well-being, ensure that your diet consists of simple, wholesome foods, such as organic produce, fresh fruit, and vegetables. This will be reflected in your dreams and their symbology will be simpler and easier to interpret.

Cycles and seasons

*E*verything in the universe runs in seasons and cycles: the day, the lunar month, the year, and so on. Everything has a beginning, a middle, and an end, and observation of the cycles and seasons in dreams can help you better understand what a dream is trying to tell you.

Everything in life undergoes a process of birth, growth, fruition, and death. Death is not something to be feared, however, because after death once again comes birth. There are many correspondencies in the cycles of development, and our ancestors represented these cycles in the sign for the medicine wheel.

The symbol of the medicine wheel depicts the four points of the compass and the cycle of the seasons. This symbol was used in many cultures to represent the cycle of life.

The medicine wheel represents the circular motion of life, while the four points of the compass represent the four directions and their corresponding meanings. There are many different types of medicine wheels, but as an example we will look in the following text at the Celtic medicine wheel.

The east

The east represents the season of spring; the moon from new to its first quarter; the sunrise; and birth. Spring is the time when new life comes to the land. Plants begin to send out new shoots, and new leaves form on the trees that have been barren throughout the winter. The east is the place of inspiration and new beginnings. If you have a dream in which the time is morning, the moon is in its first quarter, or it is spring, this represents some form of initiation or beginning in your life.

The south

The south represents the summer season; the moon from its first quarter to full moon; noon; and childhood. It symbolizes a time of great activity when the energies of the universe are at their most agitated. We are able to see this purely through observation. Summer is the season when insects and many other animals are at their most industrious. The days are longer and therefore we are able to achieve a great deal during the daylight hours. It has also been noted that children are generally more hyperactive around the full moon, and admission to mental institutions is always greatest around the time of a full moon. All of these metaphors in dreams represent development or movement in one form or another.

The west

The west represents the season of fall; the moon from full to its third quarter; the setting of the sun; and adulthood. It is a time of fruition and harvest, when the fruits of our labors during the past busy months of summer are gathered in. This happens not only in nature, but also in our own development of thoughts and ideas. All of these metapohrs are symbolic of maturity. Seeds represent birth, flowers represent development, and fruit represents maturity. This progression happens everywhere in the universe, both within our own beings and in the world at large.

The north

The north represents winter; the moon from its third quarter to its dark phase; the nighttime; and death. It is a time of introspection and preparation for the birth of new ideas. It often represents the dying of old ideas, or letting go of negative thought forms. Death is something to embrace, because after it comes life and it is only by letting go of the past that you can embrace the present and walk forward into a bright future.

In life we often tend to stop the natural progress of things. We frequently resist change, when it is as inevitable as the rising of the sun each day. It is only by embracing change that we are able to make progress as human beings. If cycles or seasons appear in your dreams, be sure to take special note of them, because they are usually pointers to areas of your life where change or development needs to take place. We live in an ever-changing universe – trying to resist change goes against the laws of the universe and will inevitably lead to frustration, unhappiness, and ill-health.

Prophetic dreams

Prophetic dreams do occur. There is so much anecdotal evidence about them that they cannot be dismissed as sheer fantasy or illusion, but how does one tell when a dream is prophetic?

In general, dreams should never be taken literally. Invariably their imagery is metaphorical and should be viewed in that way. Some people do have prophetic dreams, but they are extremely rare. Such dreams are usually easy to distinguish from other dreams because their realism makes them stay in the mind in a manner that is quite distinctive.

When I was a young man, I was working as a general manager for a company that was motivated by greed. I was very unhappy in my work and eager to seek other employment. The hours were long and the company seemed only interested in exploiting its staff and customers. One night I had a dream that was different from all other dreams I had experienced. I dreamed that I got up in the morning, got dressed, and went to work as normal. When I arrived at work, however, my boss called me upstairs to his office and said that unfortunately, due to various circumstances, he would have to lay me off. I remember feeling relieved and even joyful in my dream, because I was being freed from a very dissatisfying and frustrating job.

When I woke, the dream was still very clear in my mind. I got up, dressed, and went to work as normal. As soon as I arrived at work my boss called me up to his office, and I knew exactly what was going to happen. He told me that I would have to be laid off, using exactly the words he had said in my dream. I was so amazed at the time that my dream was coming true that I remained calm and showed no sign of shock – had I not just had the dream, this would have been totally unexpected. I knew within myself that ultimately this would lead to a better life for me. With hindsight, I can now say that the loss of my job was one of the best things that ever happened to me, because it gave me an opportunity to seek a more satisfying and fulfilling life.

Prophetic dreams can prepare you for the worst and can often lead to better opportunities – they frequently provide the motivation you need to seek new opportunities.

OMENS IN DREAMS

In different societies throughout the world there are different images that, when they appear in dreams, seem to have the same meaning. In Burundi, in central Africa, for instance, dreaming of eating meat or marrow means that someone you know will soon die and be buried. Another African tribe, the Hausa, believes that if you dream that you are sitting alone and passersby do not take any notice of you, it means you will soon die. Death omens in dreams change, depending on which part of the world you visit. In Brazil, if you dream of losing a tooth it too means that someone you know is going to die.

Dreaming of death omens may seem macabre and something to fear, but the people who understand these omens also understand that death is an inevitable part of life and should not be feared. Without death we would have no appreciation of the value of living on this remarkable planet. Incidentally, it seems a widespread belief that if you actually dream of someone close to you dying, it means the very opposite: it signifies that they will almost certainly have a long and healthy life.

Complex dreams and abstract symbols

Dreams are rarely straightforward and it can often take some unraveling to understand their meaning, especially if they contain a variety of different images, as the following extract from a dream diary clearly shows:

"I was taking a rail journey and going through the ticket barriers, being given different sorts of tickets. At the last barrier I was in a hurry, but the ticket collector kept on questioning me about my route and I told him that I was heading to Edinburgh, Scotland. The ticket collector then asked if I was coming back the same day and I told him I had to, since I was on business. All of a sudden I realized that I was dressed casually, as if I were on vacation rather than on a business trip.

Suddenly whistles were blowing and we were being hurried onto the train – I caught a train going to Cardiff in Wales! I looked out of the window and we were running alongside a narrow gorge. I saw a young man running downhill. He slipped over, got up, looked behind him, and then ran off again. I saw that he was being pursued by other men.

I was then no longer in the train, but in a street looking toward the cross-section of a T-junction. The young man had been caught, and was being hit and was in obvious pain. I wanted to do something and a girl said to me, "Call the police." I walked toward the T-junction and saw a phone booth, but a woman in a yellow dress was using it. The men left the young man and I felt that I was at risk, if they knew what I planned to do, so I pretended to look in the stores.

I saw a gift store and noticed that there was a telephone wire going to it. I went in and asked if I could phone the police. The woman in the store said that she would do so, but then seemed to delay making the call. I told her it was urgent, to which she replied, "What if all his teeth are knocked out? The police won't be able to help him then." I left the store and heard a bell ringing and thought it was a police car, but a van drove into view with the word 'Maintenance' written on it."

Analyzing complex dreams

Whenever you try to understand a dream, try to look at it from different angles. The previous dream has a general theme of anxiety and helplessness. The dreamer is trying to get somewhere, but is repeatedly delayed and then gets on the wrong train. This may well be a comment on the dreamer's life – wanting to achieve goals, but finding himself sidetracked or blocked. Wearing the wrong clothes is indicative of a lack of preparedness, which may be part of the reason why goals cannot successfully be achieved.

The dreamer seems to want to help the victim but is lacking the resources. The victim is almost certainly another metaphor for the dreamer's own life. The woman wearing the yellow dress may be an indication that the dreamer's intellectual mind is failing to find a simple resolution to the problems presented in the dream. The woman in the store offers another "unproductive" thought. This leads to the image of a maintenance van, perhaps because the victim needs his teeth maintaining – or perhaps this may be just another intellectual red herring.

Catching the wrong train, inappropriate dress, the woman in the telephone booth – again these distractions and delays show that the dreamer's goal is even further out of reach. The appearance of the maintenance van is an indicator that something in the dreamer's life may need support or repair.

Distortions of reality in dreams

To interpret dreams you must understand that words and images absorbed by the subconscious mind can reemerge as seemingly bizarre scenarios or subjects in your dreams. For instance, reading about or seeing a field during your waking hours could reappear in a dream about W.C. Fields or Gracie Fields.

*D*reams are rarely what they seem at face value. The mind makes complex associations, which sometimes have to be unraveled before the dream becomes clear. What seems strange in this reality is perfectly normal in the ever-changing world of dreams, which our minds create moment by moment and replay to us each night.

Whenever a bizarre or abstract object or subject appears in your dreams, the first thing to look at is how you describe it. This is because the mind often distorts words and meanings in order to create the dream. For instance, one of my dream diarists is a vicar. He had been studying the Old Testament and reading the Book of Ruth. It tells the story of a woman named Ruth who, due to great hardship, asks some farmers if she can pick up any grain that has been left behind by the harvesters. A man named Boaz sees her and is so taken by her that he allows her to harvest from his field. In the translation that the vicar was studying he read that Ruth found *grace* in the eyes of Boaz who told her to stay in his *field* and not look at any other field. Shortly afterward, the vicar dreamed about being interviewed by Gracie Fields.

The mind can take two seemingly unrelated words, such as grace and field, and from them make an association with the famous star Gracie Fields. The mind then uses that character in the creation of a dream. In such circumstances you can recognize why the character has appeared in the dream and can ignore its "bizarreness." This will then allow you to look at what is actually going on in the dream and what its significance is.

Sometimes you may find it impossible to figure out how your mind has conjured up the characters who enter your dream world, but this should not sidetrack you from looking deeper into what is occurring in the dream and from discovering what it is trying to tell you.

The mind does not lose its capacity for humor during a dream – puns are commonplace. One diarist dreamed of a woman fishing for something in the river – her name was Annette!

Fun and humor in dreams

Not all dreams have deep, complex meanings. Some are very simple; many contain humorous aspects. Puns are especially common in dreams. These are all signs of the mind's wonderful depth and variety, as the following examples from dream diaries illustrate:

A lady is in a river up to her neck. She is looking for something and her name is Annette. (The woman is clearly fishing for something and has a name that sounds like a net.)

Three cartoon aardvarks are walking on their back legs, dressed as three judges. One aardvark is saying, "We always wanted to do this." (This relates to a story the dreamer read about a judge who passed a death sentence because he always wanted to say the words! The dreamer had no idea why the aardvarks were in the dream.)

Somebody came up to me and asked me how to keep out of trouble, to which I replied, "I believe in being cool, calm, and cowardly!"

Dreams can also be lighthearted. One dreamer had been reading about a judge but had no idea why three comical aardvarks dressed as judges appeared in his dream.

There are no rules

*E*veryone is unique, so it follows that everyone's perception of the land of dreams will be different. In effect, you create your own reality in the land of dreams. Ultimately there are no rules.

Understanding dreams is an art that is unique to every individual. No one can tell you what your dreams mean; the answers lie within you. The only way to work successfully with your dreams is to have an honest desire to grow spiritually and emotionally. If you refuse to look at the truth within yourself, then your dreams – like your life – will be only an illusion.

Accurate interpretation of your dreams comes with practice, not through endless reading and studying of the meanings of symbols. The more you work with your dreams, the clearer they will become to you. All it takes is patience and perseverance, coupled with that desire to grow. Understanding your dreams will help you to improve the quality of your life. The more you work on yourself, the closer you will get to realizing the life of your dreams. It is possible to bring dreamtime into the reality of our everyday lives.

Faith, doubt, and determination

In order to work successfully with your dreams and achieve true happiness in life you need the following three attributes:

Faith – you need to believe that dreams have value and are, in one sense, real. You also need the faith to believe that if you begin to delve into your subconscious, it will make you a better, wiser, and stronger person. This is true, but you must believe it yourself.

Doubt – always question things in life. Never simply accept another person's word about what your dreams mean. Looking up the meanings of symbols and accepting them at face value as relating directly to your dream will teach you nothing at all. Sometimes the meaning of a symbol in a dream is unique to you and your perception of the world.

Determination – if you keep working with this path, you will learn to walk toward the life of your dreams. Tread the path of determination and never let go of your dreams – they are unique to you and an important part of you.

SUMMARY OF DREAM ANALYSIS

When analyzing your dreams, look for the following:

• Previous associations: does your dream relate to something you have experienced before, either in real life or in another dream?

• Themes: do your dreams have themes – that is, do the same emotions (e.g. anxiety, anger, fear) or occurrences (e.g. flying, running, falling) appear in several dreams?

• Puns and distortions: are parts of your dream created through word association, puns, or distortions of events that you have witnessed in life, read, or seen on television?

• Characters and symbols: do your dreams all revolve around you, children, the opposite sex, pets or other animals, your place of work, or a place from your past?

• The message of the dream: all dreams convey some sort of message – try to look for this. It is unlikely that you will initially find messages in all your dreams, but the longer you work with them, the more such messages will reveal themselves to you. If the message is to take some form of action, you will be foolish to do nothing. Act upon your dreams.

PART THREE *Living in your dreams*

If somebody tells you that dreams are just for children, they are wrong. Dreams are for everyone. It is your birthright as a human being to live in your dreams. All you have to do is claim that birthright.

The final section of this book seeks to tell you how to feel happy, healthy, and fulfilled every moment of every day. To live in your dreams is merely an attitude of mind, so it can be achieved in the time it takes to think a thought — but it is that simplicity that eludes people. Each page of this section contains different versions of the same truth, put in lots of different ways to help you to see it. If you can grasp the concepts set out here, you will have a key to unlocking the door to the life of your dreams.

What does living in your dream mean?

Living in your dreams means living the life of your dreams, where you feel happy, healthy, and fulfilled 24 hours a day, 365 days of the year. If you think this is an impossible dream, think again. As soon as you choose to believe that having a happy, healthy, and fulfilling life is impossible, it will become impossible for you to achieve. You have to believe it 100 percent and work with maximum determination to make it a living reality in your everyday life.

This is about changing the way you think and approach life. Happiness is just an attitude, a way of perceiving things. You can go to the richest parts of the world and find misery. Equally, you can go to the poorest parts and find people who are happy. True happiness is not dependent upon anything or anyone, and the same is true of unhappiness. You choose to be happy or sad — no one makes you that way. Even if somebody is really negative toward you, you still have a choice in how you react.

Only you have the power to make yourself happy or sad. If you understand this, you will also understand that, once you find true happiness, no one can take it away from you. Living the life of your dreams means owning the kind of happiness that is totally independent of anyone or anything. It can be found by anyone — anywhere — and from any background.

Bringing dreamtime into reality

Dreamtime is real and powerful. It is a rich resource of insight and inspiration that can empower you with the life of your dreams.

It is possible to bring dreamtime into this reality in which we live and work. This does not mean that you will have a fantasy life; on the contrary, it means that for the first time you will be truly living. You can have the life of your dreams, because you have the power within you to create your own reality. How you perceive the world is entirely up to you. You can choose to see it as a place full of danger, deception, and misery or as a magical place full of limitless possibilities. Both views are valid and both are correct – it is just that one view brings sadness and frustration, whereas the other brings happiness, health, and fulfillment.

As we have seen, there is no good or bad in the world until human beings interact with energy. In any given situation you always have a choice in the way you perceive it. Is losing your job a good or bad thing? It depends entirely upon how you react to that situation. If losing your job means that you grow depressed, with low self-esteem, and become a beggar on the streets or take your own life, then you will, through your choices, have made it a bad thing. If, on the other hand, it leads you to finding a better job that is much more fulfilling, then you have, through your choices, made it a good thing. The only difference between the two scenarios is in the choices that you make.

Making positive choices in your dreams serves as a blueprint for making the best out of a bad situation in your waking life. If you have fallen down a hole, you should prepare as best you can to climb out again.

MAKING CHOICES

Imagine that you are walking down a road when suddenly you fall
down a hole. You did not see the hole, so you find yourself in a
situation where you are cold, confused, and angry, and it takes a
long time for you to get out of the hole. Now imagine that you are
walking down the same street, except that this time you are aware
of the hole. You try to avoid, it but you still fall into it. You find
yourself in a situation where you are cold and angry, and it
takes you a long time to get out of the hole.
Now you walk down the street for a third time. This time you are
aware of the hole and the fact that it will be your fault if you fall
down it. You try much harder to avoid it, but still you fall down the
hole. You understand that you are totally responsible for your
situation, but still you are cold, and it takes you a long time to get
out of the hole. You now walk down the street a fourth time. This
time you are aware of the hole, aware that it is cold in the hole,
and that it is difficult to get out of; so you take a coat and an ice-ax
with you. To try to use the ax to keep yourself from falling into the
hole, but still you fall in. This time it is clear why you fell into
the hole, you are prepared, so you are not cold, and you use the
ax to get out of the hole quickly and efficiently.
I, on the other hand, would choose to walk down a different street!

Finding your dream

Most of us have lost the understanding of how to achieve happiness, health, and fulfillment. We spend much of our lives compromising our dreams, rather than living in them. We do the things that others expect us to do, rather than those things that make us truly happy. We have lost sight of our individual destiny and thus our true happiness.

So how do you reconnect with your destiny? What is your destiny? Your destiny is a path of learning where you are in harmony with the universe around you and truly feel content. To find your destiny, all you need to do is actively seek those things that make you feel happy, healthy, and fulfilled. To live in your dreams is to live your destiny.

To be happy, you have to be able to embrace everything with pleasure, and this can only truly be achieved if you are doing what you want to do. This may sound selfish, but in fact it is the only sensible way to live. All the people around you, who care about you, want you to be happy and seek happiness in their own lives. If you are happy, you will teach those around you the same contentment. If you want your children to learn how to be happy, you must first learn how to be happy. And when you connect with your destiny it is the most wonderful feeling. You know that you are in the right place, at the right time, doing the right thing. You have a sense of truly belonging and of inner peace and joy.

So what would you really like to be doing in your life? This is a question we rarely ask ourselves. Most people's dreams – the things that they really want to do – are very achievable, given the right energy and focus. Two of the most common things that prevent people from doing what they really want to do are time and money. "I would really like to do ... but I just haven't got the time" or "If I had enough money, I would be able to give up my job and ... " are two of the most frequent thoughts we have. We are content merely to fantasize about the kind of life we would really like, not realizing that it is possible for the life of our dreams to become reality if only we are willing to work for it.

We all have a common thread running through our individual destinies. We are all on this planet in order to learn. Some people think that they are here only to teach others, but in fact our focus should be only on what we have to learn. It is not your concern what others have to learn, and thinking about this simply detracts from your own learning. Every day we have an opportunity to learn lessons and thus become wiser, stronger, and better individuals. Every encounter has its teachings, if only we are willing to look for them.

Finding out what you really want to do

As we have seen, two of the main things that stop us from connecting with what we really would like to do with our lives are time and money. The following two scenarios take those elements out of the equation to give you a clearer perspective.

1. Imagine that one day you meet someone with exceptional psychic powers. This person tells you all about your life, including some things that only you knew, which you find very impressive. She then tells you about some things that are going to be happening in your life in the coming weeks and warns you of potential difficulties. Using this information makes your life run very smoothly, because you are much better prepared for what lies ahead. You form a friendship with this person and every month you meet up for a consultation about the weeks ahead. You believe everything this person tells you, because she is always completely accurate in her predictions. Then one day you meet her and she says that she has some difficult news for you. She foresees that you have only six months left to live. It does not matter what you do; you will disincarnate in six months. What would you do during those six months?

2. The next scenario begins as the previous one, except that this time you have a happy, long, and healthy life ahead of you. You meet the psychic, as before, and form a friendship with her, but this time she gives you the winning numbers to every lottery taking place in the world this month, so that you become a multi - millionaire. What would you do once you had paid all the bills, bought your friends and family presents, taken a vacation, or donated lots of money to charity?

"What would make me really happy?"

Many people think that if they had more money in their lives, it would make them happier; it would not. Having lots of money can make your life more comfortable, but cannot buy you happiness. Being comfortable is not healthy because it breeds stagnation and dissatisfaction. Canada, for instance, has low-level unemployment and a very high standard of living, yet the country has one of the highest suicide rates in the world. Clearly a high standard of living does not make everyone happy, healthy, and fulfilled. If you are too comfortable with your life, then you will never be able to find true happiness and fulfillment.

Happiness is not a limited resource

However happy you are now in your life, you can be even happier. However healthy and fulfilled you feel, your quality of life can get even better. The more you learn about living in your dreams, the happier, healthier, and more fulfilled you will become. There is no limit to the level of improvement you can achieve in the quality of your life because a high-quality life depends upon high-quality dreams. If you set your mind on a dream and achieve it, how content you will feel. But that is not the end, because as you fulfill one dream, you create a new one – going onward and forever upward on the path to ultimate freedom.

Take time to reflect on what will really make your life more fulfilled – would more money really bring you true happiness?

Fixing your dream

Now you have set your goals in mind, take one small step each day toward your dreams.

Once you have an understanding of what you would really like to do with your life, you can then begin to make that dream a reality. Taking one step at a time, you can call your dream into life.

If you did the two exercises on page 88 you should now have a list of ideas of what you would really like to do, if you did not have the constraints of time and money. This will form the foundation of your dream, because dreams are not dependent upon time or money. You have no idea what the future holds, so there is no way of predicting the course of your life. The only thing you have is a direction to travel in and that should be toward your unfolding dream, if you want to achieve happiness, health, and fulfillment.

It is possible to attract money into your life. As you journey, if you keep focused on your dream, you will attract people who will help you realize your dream and some of these people may help you financially. They may not give you money directly, but they will lead you to connections that will help you financially.

HOW TO BE FREE FROM FINANCIAL WORRIES

To be free of money worries is simply an attitude of mind. Why worry about money when you don't have it? All it does is take your energy away, thus stopping you from making efforts to effect a change in your current situation. We have all had financial worries at some time in our lives and we have all come out the other side of them. Everything has a beginning, middle, and end. The only thing you can effectively do when presented with financial difficulties is to keep treading your path of destiny. If you stop treading it, and start going around in circles with worry, you will find it much harder to connect with a solution because you will become static. To effect external change in your life, you must always effect internal change first.

Prioritizing your dream

Look at the list of "dreams" you have made and begin to prioritize them. Ask yourself which dreams are achievable in the short, middle, and long term. You will find that some of your dreams are highly achievable, by making no more than a few changes in your life, whereas others are further away from reality. Never put conditions upon your dream, such as "I want to have traveled all over the world by the time I'm 50." Dreams should not be dependent upon time.

Place your dreams in order of achievability and spend a few moments before you go to bed each night reading your list. This will program your mind with the intention of where you want your life to lead. Your subconscious will then present to you dreams that hold insights and lessons to help make those dreams a reality.

As we have already said, dreams are signposts; once you have a clear idea in your mind of where you want your life to be heading, the signposts become much easier to read.

Study your dream list each night and decide which dreams are easily achievable and which ones will take longer to realize.

91

Claiming your dream

Your dream is yours and yours alone. Nobody can take it away from you; only you can give it away. If you abandon your dream at the first obstacle that occurs, you will have missed the purpose of life.

Life's lessons

Once you have your dream fixed firmly in your mind, you have to trust that *everything* that manifests itself in your life is one stepping stone closer to that dream. There is no good or bad – only lessons. To make a dream into a reality you need to acquire new skills and improve those you already have. This can only happen if you are willing to embrace without resistance the lessons that life gives you. Life is a giant school of learning. Once you understand this you will find lessons in everything. To get to where you want to be requires movement, but the dream does not come to you – you have to find it.

Embracing change

The only constant in the universe is change, and by learning to embrace change, you will learn to flow with the energies of the universe, which are like a river that is forever flowing. Once you learn to flow with the river, it will take you

Making changes in your life is part and parcel of achieving your dream – go with the flow and do not try to resist change.

to places beyond your dreams. Your true destiny is your dream and it is the path of least resistance. The more you learn to "go with the flow," the farther that flow will take you – you should resist nothing and embrace everything.

Thinking clearly

We spend much of our lives thinking about things that are of no relevance. Holding on to the past or worrying about the future both represent unhealthy thinking and a waste of energy.

How much of what is in your mind at the moment would cease to be relevant if you knew that the world was going to end in 48 hours? If that were the case, so many things would cease to be relevant. People who have wronged or hurt you would no longer be worth thinking about. All your anger, resentment, and pain would have no further relevance. All concerns about the future would disappear, and you would be left with thoughts of "How can I be happy in the next two days?" This is how your thinking should be all the time. Live in the present. Leave the past behind and do not worry about the future. By not worrying about it, you will create a brighter future for yourself.

Keeping faith with your dream

Like everything in life, your unfolding dream runs in cycles. There will be times when the path is easy and other times when the path is hard, but as long as you keep walking along the path you will achieve your dream.

Embracing life's challenges

A life that is easy all the time is a boring life that leads to stagnation and unhappiness. Life needs to be challenging at times, because it is precisely those challenges that teach and empower us most. Life only becomes hard when you try to avoid or ignore those challenges. Every obstacle you meet in life represents a challenge for you to overcome and in the process become wiser and stronger. There is no hurdle that cannot be surmounted, although sometimes you need to learn patience before obstacles can truly be mastered. The greatest obstacles in life will come, not from other people, but from within yourself. If you look for the positive in everything, life will become easier for you. If you always look on the dark side, your life will be beset by endless trials and tribulations.

The art of traveling light

Someone who is traveling with two heavy suitcases and a large knapsack is inevitably going to find any journey much harder than someone who has no baggage. The same is true on the path toward your dreams. If you hold on to the past you will be carrying a lot of emotional baggage, which will make the going tough and some obstacles insurmountable. To be empowered on your path you have to let go of all this baggage. This means releasing all your hurt, pain, anger, resentment, and jealousy, for it is of no importance to you anyway. All the time you hold on to it you hold on to unhappiness. Let it go and you will feel lighter and brighter, and a lot closer to your dream.

The path that takes you to the life of your dreams is strewn with all kinds of challenges, but it is in overcoming these obstacles that you strengthen your resolve to attain your dream. The lessons will help you grow as a person.

WISHING CEREMONY

If, at any time in your life, you feel as if you are losing sight of your

dream, a simple wishing ceremony can help you refocus your mind.

Write down on a piece of paper how you want your life to change

for the better; write down your intentions for the future.

This can include listing the things you recognize that you need to let

go of, as well as the things that you want to attract into your life

as part of your unfolding dream.

Once you have written down your "wishes," light a candle and read

your wishes to yourself three times. Each time you read them,

visualize the energy of your thoughts and dreams going out to the far

corners of the universe. Now fold the piece of paper and set fire

to it using the candle. As the paper burns, visualize the smoke as

all your dreams and wishes traveling heavenward.

You can also perform this ceremony outside. The more energy you put

into the ceremony, the more powerful it will be for you. You may want

to light a small fire outside instead of a candle, and you can also

create a miniature altar to act as a focal point for your ceremony.

Decorate the altar with flowers, crystals, and other naturally beautiful

things and use it every time you feel the need to

refocus on your dream.

Changing perspective

*A*ny problem that you have is only a problem because of the way in which you are perceiving it. A solution is just a problem viewed from a different perspective. The power of changing perspective is the power of problem-solving.

Focusing on solutions

In the modern Western world we tend to be much more focused on problems than on solutions. The strategy of most therapists and counselors is to try to get to the root of problems by getting their patients to recount their problems. But in many cases a problem shared can be a problem doubled. The best thing to do is to focus on solutions. Rather than asking what the problem is, ask yourself what kind of solution you would like. If you are not happy with a part of your life, rather than focus on what is making you unhappy, ask yourself, "How would I like my life to be?" This will show you the direction you need to take to get the solution that you seek.

If you cannot see a solution to a problem when you are awake, you can use dreamtime to find the solution. Before you go to sleep, program your subconscious mind to work on the problem (*see* page 108). Do this simply by thinking "I want my subconscious mind to be working on this problem while I am asleep." If you then program yourself to remember and record your dreams, you will often find that a new perspective emerges, which in turn leads you toward a solution.

If you carry out this presleep programming, your dreams will give you the signposts. All you have to do is read

them. It is a bit like being stuck in a traffic jam. When you have a problem for which you can find no solution, the conscious mind acts like someone in an automobile, unable to see more than a couple of vehicles ahead or behind. The perspective is too narrow for you to be able to see a way out. Dreamtime takes you out of the vehicle and shows you an image of where you have been and how to find a way out quickly and efficiently. Once you understand how to read the map, the solution manifests itself in your conscious mind.

Conflict resolution

Sometimes in life we come into conflict with others. Such conflicts can have a detrimental effect on our progress toward our dream if we do not handle them correctly.

Conflicts are no more or less than communication and perspective differences. Whenever you get into a conflict with another person it is always because either you do not fully understand each other or you have two different perspectives on the same issue. The best way to resolve this is to understand the other person's perspective and his or her manner of communication. You can do this by using a version of the repetition exercise on page 31.

Think of a recent occasion when you have been in conflict with another person. You are going to replay that conflict three times in your mind. The first time, review it from your own perspective, taking special note of the other person: his or her body language, gestures, words, and tone of voice. Using this information, replay the conflict a second time from the other person's perspective. This will give you a new set of information. Using all of this information, replay the conflict a third time from an outside perspective, as if you were viewing it from afar. You should now have a clear understanding of the other person's point of view and a better idea of how to resolve the conflict.

Conflicts with colleagues or friends only serve to hinder you on the path toward your goal. Dream techniques enable you to see a problem from several perspectives and find a mutually acceptable solution.

Trials and tribulations

Making simple changes in your life, such as streamlining your closet and getting rid of unnecessary clutter, educates the mind to seek an uncomplicated approach to dealing with life's challenges.

*I*n life there are always difficulties, but the way in which you handle them will have a marked effect on how long they last and how much they affect you. The successful resolution should leave you feeling wiser, better, and stronger.

When they come across difficulties and hardships, many people try to use food or other external stimuli to make themselves feel better. They comfort-eat or take drugs, filling their bodies with complex chemicals that cloud their minds and judgment. Such measures only serve to make their difficulties last even longer. When life becomes complicated by trials and tribulations there are two things that will ensure you get a quick resolution:

Simplify your life

When faced with hardship, the first thing to do is simplify things. Put aside all matters that it is not essential to think about at the present time. Use the "world ending in 48 hours" analogy on page 93. The less complicated your thinking is, the more quickly you will find a solution. All solutions are simple. The more simply you think, the easier life will become.

Initiate change

When a situation is "stuck," the only way to move things on is by initiating change. Simplifying your diet will help to change your perspective, but you can alter many other aspects of your life as well. Change your routines and habits, your clothes, rest time, social activities, or anything else you can. By changing things, your thinking and your perspectives on life will alter and resolutions will manifest themselves.

THE POWER OF FASTING

Fasting is one of the most powerful ways of changing your perspective and connecting with solutions. But because it has great power for good, fasting can do an equal amount of harm if not done with common sense. Most people (except those with medical problems, such as diabetes) can safely go without food for a day or two. An even safer way to fast is just to eat one simple wholefood. This gives your body all the nutrients it needs, but, because you are eating only one food, it allows you all the mental benefits of fasting. Short-grain organic brown rice is the best grain to fast with, because it contains virtually all the nutrients your body needs. It does not contain vitamin B12, but since it takes five years to become deficient in this vitamin, fasting on rice for only a few days will do you no harm at all.

You can fast on rice alone for one to four days without supervision, but longer fasts should always be undertaken with the guidance of a qualified practitioner. The more simply you eat, so the easier it is to find solutions to problems and difficulties, since your thinking is also simplified.

Finding the positive in everything

In any situation there is something positive to be found. In fact, the worse the situation, the greater the good that can come out of it. The key is looking for that positive thing and finding it in everything.

There are many situations that we *view* as negative, but that is only one view. There is always a positive side, if you search for it. Suppose a friend comes to you and asks to borrow some money. You can only afford to lend it to your friend for three days, and he assures you that he will pay you back in full within that time, so you lend it to him. Every time you see him, he says that he will repay you, but one month later you still have not had any money from him. Is this a positive or negative situation? It depends on how you react to it. Look at the two reactions below and you will see that you always have a choice in how you react.

Negative reaction

You become angry with your "friend." You feel that he has let you down and put you in a very difficult situation. You have got into debt and are having to work hard to find the money you need, and this only adds to your frustration. Every time you see the other person it reminds you how he has cheated and betrayed you, and that makes you even angrier. You become very unhappy and say to yourself, "That is the last time I am ever going to lend anyone any money, because people cannot be relied upon to keep their word. I will never be able to trust anyone again." You become disillusioned with life and stop trusting all your friends. You end up very bitter and lonely.

Positive reaction

You recognize that you are 100 percent responsible for losing the money. You understand that it was your lack of judgment that led you into this situation, so you embrace the extra work you have to do, without anger or resentment. You look hard within yourself to find out what lessons you have to learn. You say to yourself, "That is the last time I'm ever going to lend anyone any money, because people cannot be relied upon to keep their word. Instead, whenever anyone asks me to lend him or her money, I will ask myself whether I can afford to *give* that person the money. If I can, I will give it with total pleasure, seeking nothing in return except the enjoyment of giving."

The negative response is that of an arrogant individual, who thinks he or she has little to learn. The positive response is that of an enlightened person who understands that there is positive to be found in everything. The positive response puts you in a situation where you do not need to become angry. You have given a gift with love and sought nothing in return. But by doing that you have sent out a positive energy, which will reap rich rewards for you in terms of your happiness, health, and fulfillment.

If the person returns the money, then that is a bonus. If he or she does not, then the universe will reward you in another way. "As you sow, so shall you reap."

Try to react positively to a negative situation. If you've had a bad experience lending someone money, see it as a lesson and resolve to lend somebody money only if you can afford to give that person the money. When the money is returned it will seem like an unexpected bonus.

Keeping the dream

When life is tough and you feel lonely and isolated, remember your dream. Change your thinking and focus your mind firmly on your goals. Walk onward and upward with the assurance that you are claiming your right to happiness, health, and fulfillment.

To appreciate day, you must
experience night.
To appreciate joy, you must experience pain.
To understand the meaning of health,
you must first become ill.
To find fulfillment,
you must first hunger for it.

Everything comes to teach you, and there is no good or bad until you interact with those things that come to challenge you. If you never lose sight of these truths, you will never lose sight of your dream. Keeping your dream means keeping faith with yourself. When challenges arise, remind yourself why you are on this path and where you are heading. Remember that everything has a beginning, middle, and end and that, provided you keep treading your path with humility and a desire to learn, there are no challenges that cannot be mastered.

If you truly understand that everything comes to teach you, you will be able to say genuinely, from your heart, "Welcome hardship," "Welcome pain," and "Welcome aversion." You will be able to embrace everything with equal pleasure – from a sumptuous banquet to a bowl of plain brown rice, from joy to pain. In order to achieve this state you must walk the middle path of balance and harmony. A state of euphoria is as imbalanced as depression. Eating a very strict diet all your life is as bad for you as constantly eating junk food. Look for the middle ground in everything. Hold on to nothing and reject nothing and you will find freedom beyond

Walk tall on the path to your dream. Rise above the most difficult challenges and keep hold of your dream.

your dreams. You must find peace in everything and understand that you must learn to view with pleasure those things in life that you cannot change.

> *It is not miserable to be blind;*
> *it is miserable to be incapable*
> *of enduring blindness.*

Goal reviewing

As you progress on the path toward your dreams, you and the world around you will inevitably change, so it is a good idea to review your dreams at least once a year. You may find that some of the things you thought would be important have faded into insignificance, whereas other things have become more important. Review all the goals on your original dream list and check to see whether they are still in the correct order of achievability.

You might like to repeat the exercises that take the elements of time and money out of the equation and see whether the two scenarios given on page 88 produce the same answers. Your ultimate aim is to

be able to say, "If I suddenly became rich, or if I knew I only had six months to live, I would do nothing different from what I am doing now. I am happy, healthy, and fulfilled. What more could I need?"

You might also like to repeat the wishing ceremony (*see* page 95) as a means of reaffirming your commitment to your unfolding dream. Dreams should never be set in stone. As you yourself change, your perspective on life will alter and so will your dream. This is why it is called an unfolding dream, because it should never end. Our dreams should be forever expanding, like the universe that we inhabit.

Remember that going to extremes in any walk of life is unproductive. Maintaining a balance in all things will keep you grounded and focused on achieving your goal.

Advanced learning

By sending out pure thoughts that he wished to learn to play the bodhran, the author's subconscious took in all the information from a television program and later brought it together to enable his conscious mind to understand how to play this instrument.

You have the ability to create your own reality and to manifest things in your life. This is not an easy skill to acquire, although it is quite simple to do.

Learning new skills

I was given an Irish drum called a bodhran (pronounced bough-rawn) as a present and decided that I would like to learn to play it. I was seeking to play purely for pleasure and to honor the person who gave me the present. I tried to play it, but with little success; so I sent a thought to the universe that I would like to learn how to play this beautiful drum. When I found that I could not play it I was not disappointed: I just recognized that I needed to acquire the skills to play it. This meant that my thought was untarnished by emotion; it was just a thought.

About two months later, by sheer chance, I came across a television program in which the presenter was using the Internet to help her learn to play the bodhran. I watched it for the next half-hour as she received advice from various Websites on how to play the bodhran.

About a month later, I was listening to some Irish music and on one track there was a bodhran playing. As I listened to it I suddenly realized that I knew how to play the bodhran. So I picked up my drum and began to play it, as if it were quite natural to me. I received no actual lessons – it just came to me.

Put out a pure thought and wait, with faith, for it to become a reality. Provided the thought is pure and you embrace all experience with an open mind, it will come back to you. Simply think, watch, be patient, and trust.

MASTERING THE EGO

When you send out pure thoughts, untarnished by emotion, to the universe, that energy comes back to you purely and efficiently. To be able to send out pure thoughts you must have mastered the ego. It is the ego that says "I desire this," "I deserve that," and "It's not fair," but all these thoughts come from a perspective of selfishness and self-centeredness. In order to be able to create your own reality you must send out selfless thoughts that are completely untarnished by emotion. This does not mean that you have no thoughts for yourself; it means that you do not place yourself at the heart of those thoughts.

If you desire things so that people will think better of you or so that you can increase your pride, then you will not find the satisfaction with life that everyone is seeking. Your thoughts must be pure. When you send out your dreams into the universe you must do so with total nondependence. This means that you are not depending on the dream coming true for your personal happiness. You have to find satisfaction with your present life before you can successfully manifest other things in your life.

Exploring the dark side

A man who fears suffering is already suffering from what he fears.

To be truly happy, healthy, and fulfilled requires you to find inner peace, free from fear. This can only come when you look at yourself honestly and openly. We all have a "dark side." It consists of the parts of ourselves that we seek to hide from others. We often feel that if people knew what we were really like, they would not like us. What this means is that there are areas of our lives that cause us to dislike ourselves. The answer is to change those negatives to positives, but this can only be achieved through honest introspection. Looking at the darker side of our nature, our inner fears, and our weaknesses is not a pleasant task, but once they are mastered we can have a life free from fear.

*Failure is not falling down;
it is not getting back up again.*

Mastering our inner fears comes with practice and perseverance, but one of the chief stumbling blocks for people on the journey to self-improvement is fear of failure. If you learn from your mistakes, and pick yourself up each time you fall down, then it becomes impossible for you to fail. Failure is only an attitude of mind. When you fall down in life, this is a wonderful opportunity for you to learn, if you choose to see it that way. If you are open to learning from everything, then fear of failure becomes a thing of the past. Every time you learn from a mistake, you make sure that you will never repeat that mistake again. You will have become a wiser, better, and stronger person as a result of that mistake. This will happen only if you look honestly at your failings, rather than trying to hide them from yourself and from those around you.

Learning to let go

You choose to hold on to pain and anger; equally you can choose to let go of them. However, holding on to pain and anger is not usually a conscious choice, but a subconscious one. Whenever we find ourselves in a situation where we lose our power to another person, we subconsciously seek to gain something in return. Most of the time what we exchange for our power is pain and anger – but we do not have to hold on to this, we can choose to let it go.

Much of the time the ego says, "I deserve to have this pain and anger, because I've been wronged," so you cling to it. If you recognize that you attract

Pain and anger are negative emotions that can fester inside you. Learning to let go of these feelings will make you a stronger person.

everything into your life in order to learn, you can simply choose to let go of negative emotions and concentrate instead on making sure that you do not attract another similar negative situation into your life. This "letting go" is hard for people to do only because they have not mastered their own egos. However, if you let the ego go, with it will go all these disempowering emotions.

Dreams and programming

Your mind is active 24 hours a day and you can make it work for you all the time, even when you are asleep.

The mind is a wonderful thing – it works on many different levels and is constantly busy. If you have a problem to which your conscious mind cannot find a solution, your subconscious keeps working on the problem long after it has left the conscious mind. If the subconscious finds a solution, it then tells it to the conscious mind and we experience this as a sudden realization. Nearly everyone has experienced this phenomenon at some time in their lives, but you can use this skill on a nightly basis.

Dreams give you access to the subconscious mind, and you can use this area to resolve problems and find insights while you are sleeping.

How to program your dreams

If you have a problem or unresolved issue that you want your subconscious mind to work on while you are asleep, all you have to do is mentally ask your mind to ponder the problem and to give you a solution or a new perspective to it. Then put all conscious thoughts concerning the problem out of your mind and let your subconscious get to work.

You may find that if you remember your dreams that night, they will provide you with clues and insights. You may also find that you wake up with new thoughts or ideas that were not in your conscious mind when you went to sleep.

I use this technique when I am not clear what to write about. I tell my mind the subject I am researching and ask it to give me some thoughts and ideas to develop. The following morning I always find that I wake up with lots of new ideas. I do not have to do any complex meditation, for the ideas are already formulated in my conscious mind. There is nothing magical about this – it is simply utilizing a talent that lies dormant within all of us.

A WORD OF WARNING

If you use this technique to help you solve problems, it is very important that, once you have asked the mind to work on the problem while you sleep, you put all thoughts of it from your conscious mind. Otherwise you will spend all night thinking about the problem, instead of getting restful sleep and dreaming the answer. This takes mental discipline but it is not difficult to do if you remember the following:

If you cannot consciously find an answer to a problem, it is a waste of time and energy to let it dominate your waking thoughts.

Let your subconscious mind do the work for you.

You must have faith in your own ability to dream solutions to your problems or you will not be able to let it go in your mind and it will stop you from having a good night's sleep.

Before you go to sleep, think of something positive and beautiful. Let go of all stress and worry. Letting go is merely a choice that you make; it is not difficult unless you choose to make it so.

Learning total acceptance

Total acceptance is an attitude of mind. If you hold on to nothing and reject nothing, you can never be hurt or disappointed and you will always feel content.

How not to give away your happiness

If you hold on to anger or pain, it means that you are forever in danger of giving your happiness away to other people. This is because people can "push your buttons" and bring out that anger or pain, leaving you powerless to prevent this. Holding on to any negative emotion will potentially put you in the same situation. No one can make you angry or hurt you – only you choose to get angry or be hurt. This is a hard truth for people to grasp, but all the time you choose not to see it you are simply a victim of fate, never knowing who will "rob" you of your happiness.

How to make other people happy

It is actually impossible to make another person happy. True happiness comes only from within. If you compromise your own happiness for the sake of others, you are only teaching them how to compromise their own happiness. You should seek only your own happiness, because once you have found it, for yourself

Other people will activate your "anger button" or "pain button" only if you allow them to. True contentment lies in choosing to react positively to negative situations.

and by yourself, you can then teach others how to do the same. How can you ever hope to make other people happy if you are not happy yourself? This does not mean that you become selfish. On the contrary, you become more giving. The difference is that you learn to give, seeking nothing in return except the pleasure of giving.

If you cannot do something for another person with total pleasure, seeking nothing in return, then you should not do it. If you ignore this advice, you compromise your own happiness. If you learn to embrace and do everything with pleasure, your life will very quickly be happy, healthy, and fulfilled. This is the true meaning of unconditional love. It is all-embracing and all-encompassing.

How low self-esteem stops happiness

People with low self-esteem fall into two categories: they are either selfish or pleasers. Selfish people are under the illusion that they can find happiness by doing only what they want to do, instead of learning to do everything with pleasure.

Pleasers are those who only do what they think will make other people happy, at the expense of their own happiness. Both types are on a path to illness and misery. Some people encompass both types by being pleasers to everyone they meet and selfish at home, or vice versa.

These types need to learn to embrace everything in life with total pleasure. There is no real pleasure in being selfish toward others or being a sacrificial lamb to everyone. You should never compromise your own happiness and, if you learn to embrace everything with pleasure, you never will. You will have self-esteem and, with it, the life of your dreams.

Different perspectives

There are two ways of looking at every situation – learn to look at things from a positive perspective for a more fulfilling life.

*T*here are always two ways of looking at everything. However you view life, there is always an opposite perspective.

Changing your perspective

When difficulties occur in life, many people ask themselves the question, "Why me?" A better question to ask yourself would be "Why not me?" No one is more special than anyone else. Why should your life not have trials and difficulties, in the same way as everyone else? Besides, it is only through overcoming these obstacles in life that we learn to grow as spiritual beings. Life is a rich tapestry of experiences, all of which have the potential to be positive, if you choose to ignore self-pity and change your perspective.

When you do not wish to read any more about this subject, you will choose to put this book down and then choose to do something else instead. It is the same when you look at life. You can choose to see the positive or to dwell on the negative. You can immerse yourself in self-pity or embrace life with pleasure, while seeking new lessons to learn. It's only ever up to you. You create your own reality because you choose the perspective from which you view your life.

Whenever you feel negative toward another human being, that feeling has nothing whatsoever to do with the other person and only to do with what lies inside you. Change your perspective and you will then unlock the power to change your life for the better.

Looking at opposites

A useful way to change your perspective is to look at the opposite view. If you are asking yourself "Why?" then change it to "Why not?" If something external makes you angry, look within yourself and you will find the true root of your anger. If something appears bad, there is always a perspective from which it can be seen as good. We often view external things as bad because we have not internally learned the lesson it was trying to teach us.

If you seek to learn something from every experience you have in life, then you will understand the power of turning

Why make things more complicated than they really are? Treat any bad experience as a positive challenge and valuable lesson for the future – you may even see the funny side.

bad into good. The more you learn, the wiser and stronger you become, and as you grow, so does your self-esteem. Life becomes a big adventure, instead of a bore, and you learn to turn tears into laughter, pain into joy, and anger into love – seeing the good in everything. All human beings have this potential within them, but the understanding of it is so simple that it eludes most of them. The more simply you learn to think, the easier your life will become. Simple does not mean stupid – it means uncomplicated. The solution to every problem is simple; it is only human beings who make it complex.

People struggle to find life outside themselves, unaware that the life they are seeking lies within.

Self-sabotage

Your biggest enemy in the struggle for the life of your dreams is your own mind. Unless you can truly master the mind, it will defeat you. You are the only person who can stop yourself from bringing dreamtime into reality.

Thinking with a clear mind

There are three states of mind, no mind, one mind, and clear mind.

No mind

The people who think in this way are victims of fate. Their minds are full of irrelevant thoughts and emotions connected with the past and future. They live in regret, dwelling on their mistakes instead of learning lessons from them. They waste their energy in thinking about endless future scenarios, not understanding that whatever they imagine will not become a reality in exactly the way they assume. The future is unwritten, and trying to predict it is futile. They are stuck and cannot progress toward their dreams for fear that they will not come true. Their own fear and negative thinking creates for them a reality that is full of fear and negativity.

One mind

The people who think with one mind are walking a path toward self-destruction. They are the type of people who are

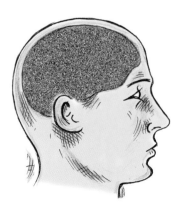 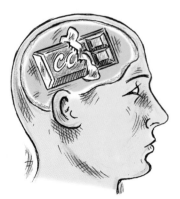 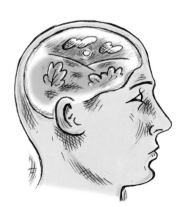

obsessive or exclusive in their thinking. They may be obsessed with food, a certain social activity, drugs, sex, or religion. They will hear only what they want to hear and will ignore the truth, even when it stares them in the face. Any path that is restrictive in the long term is not a path to happiness, health, and fulfillment. We are naturally expressive creatures and any kind of suppression is bad for us. You should hold on to nothing and reject nothing. One-minded people like to think they are open-minded, but they are actually living an illusion and will never see the whole truth.

Clear mind

The people who think with a clear mind are happy, healthy, and fufilled. They depend upon no one and take nothing personally. They understand that everything they experience they have attracted to themselves in order to learn. They embrace even the greatest hardships with total pleasure and are always looking for new lessons to learn. They eat a healthy balanced diet and are free from all addictions, because they understand that what they put into their bodies affects the quality of their thinking and their lives. They understand that the body is their temple and should be treated with honor and respect – as should everything in creation. They harbor no grudges or resentments, and view life as an adventure full of surprises and miracles.

If you want the life of your dreams, you must learn to think clearly. You must let go of everything, because by holding on to things you are stopping yourself from being free. Hold on to nothing and reject nothing. Understand that fighting a problem only compounds the problem by feeding it energy. You must learn to embrace everything in life and learn from everything. By doing so you will be drawing energy away from problems instead of feeding them energy. Once you have learned everything that a situation has to teach you, it will cease to exist in your life.

Think, think, and then think some more.

Advanced dreaming

The world of dreams is as limitless as the universe itself. There are many ways to explore it, beyond interpreting your own dreams. Once you have mastered your dreams, you may wish to explore other areas of this infinite realm.

Lucid dreaming

A lucid dream is one in which the subject is aware that he or she is dreaming and can even choose to influence the content or events of the dream. During lucid dreaming the brainstem sends out signals to the body that suppress movement and muscle activity, to minimize the chance of waking up. It is as if the brain recognizes lucid dreaming as a positive activity and does its utmost to facilitate it, once it occurs. Lucid dreaming enables you to have real interaction with your dreams. There are even reported cases of two people having "met" in their dreams when both were asleep.

Lucid dreaming can be used in a variety of ways, including for fun, for overcoming nightmares, creative thinking, problem-solving, and healing. Lucid

By using the technique of lucid dreaming, individuals can influence events in their dream. It is quite possible for two people sleeping separately to meet in their dreams.

dreaming and healing is an especially powerful combination, and many people learn to fill their dreams with positive visual imagery, since this is known to lead to improved physical health. It takes some practice to learn lucid dreaming, but, once it is mastered, many people have up to four or five lucid dreams every night. Scientists have found that it is easier to learn lucid dreaming when napping, rather than during nighttime sleep, although this is a recent discovery and many people have learned to lucid dream purely through presleep programming at night.

HOW TO TEACH YOURSELF LUCID DREAMING

Dr. Stephen LaBerge, a leading researcher and writer on lucid dreaming, teaches the
MILD (Mnemonic Induction of Lucid Dreams) technique of lucid dreaming. This technique
is practiced after waking from a dream, but before returning to sleep. It has four steps:

1. Set up dream memory. Before you go to sleep, program yourself
to remember your dreams, as shown on pages 26–27.

2. Focus your intent. When you wake from a dream and have noted down
a few keywords to help you remember it, focus your intent on remembering that
you are dreaming, the next time you do so. Say to yourself, "The next time I dream,
I will remember that I am dreaming, but will not wake up." Repeat this to yourself
over and over again, like a mantra, as you fall asleep. If you find your
mind wandering, gently bring your focus back to the mantra.

3. Visualize yourself becoming lucid. As you continue to say the words over in your
mind, imagine that you are back in the dream you have just had or – if you cannot recall
that dream – any other memorable dream. Visualize yourself recognizing that you are
dreaming and looking for confirmation that it is a dream. You might be doing something
normally impossible (such as flying), meeting somebody deceased, witnessing
extraordinary occurrences, and so on. Once you have confirmed that you are
dreaming, say to yourself, "I'm dreaming," then continue your visualization.

4. Repeat steps 2 and 3 until you fall asleep.

It may take some time before you actually have a lucid dream, but with practice
you can use this technique to make all your dreams lucid, if you choose.

Dreaming for others

*T*he only way to help other people achieve the life of their dreams is by example. Actions speak louder than words. You must find the life of your dreams before you can help others to find theirs.

Owning truth

All the information given in this book is just that – information. It alone has no power to change your life. There is a difference between knowing truth and owning it. To own truth is to take information, evaluate it, and, if it is true, take that truth into your mind and let it pervade every part of your being. You cannot live the life of your dreams from Monday to Friday and then become a selfish individual on weekends. Living the life of your dreams means embracing everything that manifests itself in your life, 24 hours a day, 365 days a year. To change others you must first change yourself.

Attaining the life of your dreams is a commitment you must stick to 365 days of the year.

What is kindness?

Is it unkind to hurt somebody's feelings? Is it better to lie than to tell the truth? The answer to both questions is never. You cannot hurt anyone else's feelings – people choose to be hurt. People are only hurt by the truth, and only then if they are resistant to change and unwilling to learn from life. The kindest thing to do to anyone is to tell the truth. This does not mean that you force your opinions on everyone you meet. It means that, if someone asks your opinion, you give him or her an honest answer. Truth is the strongest mind-altering substance on the planet. If you sympathize with people or tell them lies, then you are keeping them back from happiness, health, and fulfillment. Sympathy implies that it is okay for someone to be unhappy. I disagree. Compassion and understanding are supportive and helpful emotions to enable someone to make the transition from sadness to happiness, but sympathy serves no useful purpose.

Sympathy is an unproductive emotion to offer someone in distress. Compassion and support are what the sufferer needs to put him or her back on track.

118

Changing others

You cannot change anyone except yourself. Trying to change other people is a waste of energy, just as trying to make other people happy is. If you concentrate purely on changing yourself, you will find that, as you change, so do people around you. The way they treat you will change. As you build up your self-esteem and respect, you will begin to command respect from others. The more you change your life for the better, the more those around you will alter. Sometimes people oppose change to such an extent that they choose not to be around you anymore. That is their choice and has nothing to do with you. You can be assured that you will make many new friends as you walk your path to freedom.

Understanding yourself

As you tread the path toward the life of your dreams, it is not your place to judge others, because you do not know what their destiny is. The only person that you have the ability to judge is yourself. You must understand yourself fully before

you try to show others how to understand themselves.

You should never have to preach to others – if you are walking a path of happiness and truth, other people will be able to recognize it within you and come and ask you about it. If people do not ask you about it, then it is not your place to speak. When people do ask you a question, give them a petal of truth. If they admire the petal's beauty, then you will be able to give them a whole flower. If they discard the petal or they do not even notice it, then keep your truth to yourself. In this way you will be able to remain in harmony with all.

Do not judge others; offer them a petal of truth instead. If they value the petal they will be able to appreciate the whole flower.

Expanding the dream

When you first set out your dreams, you are limited by your understanding at that time. As you walk toward your dreams, your understanding increases and therefore your dream expands.

The dog barks at the moon, the moon doesn't care.
CHINESE PROVERB

Infinite possibilities

Within the limitless expanse of the universe all of us have infinite possibilities to learn and grow. An old Asian saying states, "Satisfy only 80 percent of your hunger. Eight-tenths sustains the man, the other two-tenths sustains the doctor." There is great wisdom in these ancient words. If you eat to only 80 percent capacity, you remain always wanting more. You must apply the same rule in life; you should never look to feel fully satisfied until the day you die. However, there is an important difference between never being fully satisfied with your life and being forever dissatisfied. The difference is that dissatisfaction is the negative emotion of an individual with no mind. Always being hungry for more is the emotion of the person with a clear mind, who lives for the present.

You are only as limited as your thinking

If you believe that the life you have now is as good as it gets, then you are limiting both your life and your happiness. If a doctor tells you that you have an incurable disease, do not believe him or her. All the doctor is saying is that he does not know of a cure; but if you believe his words you will never have any hope of a cure. Hope and faith are essential if you are to find true happiness. Do not fill your life with self-limiting philosophies, but expand your mind to perceive the limitless possibilities. Create your own reality – if you can dream it, you can make it real. There are so many things that we "care" about that are of no importance. What other people think about you is of no importance; what you believe and think about yourself is the real thing you should be examining. This does

*The mind knows no bounds.
Your imagination will let
you travel to the world of
your wildest dreams.*

not mean you should ignore the opinions of others. It simply means that when you find the truth within yourself, you should not let others draw you away from it. Nor should you try to show others the truth through your words. It is your actions that will reveal it to everyone you meet. "Hold on to nothing and reject nothing" means you understand that life is forever changing and that you need to flow with the energies of the universe. Holding on to things stops that flow, while rejecting things limits your possibilities in life.

The power of imagination

Whatever your situation in life, you have the power to be free – right now. With the power of the imagination you can go anywhere and do anything. You can travel the world, explore the universe, or just sit by a beautiful lake, surrounded by forest creatures. You might feel that your body limits you, but it does not. You are limited only by your mind. If you learn to harness the power of the imagination, you can experience anything. You can even travel back in time or into a possible future.

The world dream

The world in which we live is forever changing, with some parts becoming more ordered, while others become more chaotic. Recognizing how to change yourself for the better gives you the understanding to change the world.

Sending out ripples

If you throw a stone into a pool of water, it sends ripples out in all directions. So it is with your thoughts. Every thought, every sensation sends out vibrations into the universe. Our minds are often so full of confused, contradictory thoughts that all we send out is myriad ripples that cancel each other out. When this happens, we have very little influence upon the world around us. If, however, you simplify your life, your thinking becomes much less complex, so the thoughts you send out into the universe have a much greater effect.

If you put out only beautiful, love-filled thoughts into the universe, not only will you attract more beauty into your own life, but you will bring beauty into the lives of others — and that has the power to change lives. All the great teachers of the world have tried to pass on this simple truth, yet still it seems to elude humankind. It is so simple, we fail to see it. You really do create your own reality through the power of your mind. Think beautiful thoughts and you will see the beauty in everything. Think ugly, selfish thoughts and all you will see is suffering and pain. *You are what you think.*

Keeping on growing

Every day brings you thousands of opportunities to learn and grow. Everything you experience is significant and has wisdom to impart to you. If you open your mind and quieten its chatter, you will find that each day you become wiser, better, and stronger. Growing older should mean growing wiser and more beautiful, not becoming senile and miserable. If you teach yourself to learn day by day, you will be at one with this beautiful universe that we inhabit and, no matter what your age, people will marvel at your beauty.

No wise person ever wished to be younger.

THE TEN COMMANDMENTS OF DREAMWALKING

1 Show respect for all inhabitants of the Earth.

2 Talk less, listen more.

3 Look after your body – it is the temple of the mind.

4 Criticize less, praise more.

5 Take full responsibility for all your actions.

6 **Take less, give a hundred times a hundred.**

7 Speak only truth, act only with honesty.

8 Worry less, work harder.

9 Do always what you know to be right.

10 Frown less, laugh more.

*Thinking beautiful
thoughts and looking
on life as an exciting and
enriching experience will
bring out the beauty and
happiness within you.*

Final word

*If you meet a master swordsman,
show him your sword.
If you meet a man who is not a poet,
don't show him your poems.*

Honesty and humility

If you understand and put into action the lessons contained within this book, you will be well on the path to happiness, health, and fulfillment. You must never become complacent, for the moment you do, you will lose the dream. You must remain humble and honest at all times, both toward yourself and toward those you meet. In Mexico they say that the people who hurt you the most are your soulmates. This is because they teach you the most. Remember that a comfortable life leads to stagnation. Never believe that you have "made it," because the only time you will truly have made it is when you leave this planet.

Our worst fault is our preoccupation with the faults of others. Look forever within yourself. The answers to all your questions and the solutions to all your problems lie within you. You already know everything you need to know; you have simply forgotten how to bring it to your conscious mind. This is why exploring the land of your dreams is so

Become complacent and your dream will slip from your grasp. Our dreams have much to teach us and we must never stop learning.

YOUR DESTINY

Watch your thoughts, they
become your words.

Watch your words,
they become your actions.

Watch your actions,
they become your habits.

Watch your habits,
they become your character.

Watch your character,
it becomes your destiny.

important. It gives you access to truth and understanding. By truly understanding yourself, you will understand the world around you. If you are forever criticizing or finding fault with others, you are only drawing attention away from your own shortcomings. Look within and resolve to change your weaknesses into strengths, and you will never need to find fault with others. We are all human and none of us is perfect. No one is better or worse than you – that person is just different.

A serious choice

If you choose to embrace the truths within this book, you should do it for yourself, and by yourself, seeking nothing in return except happiness, health, and fulfillment. Understand that deciding to follow this path may well be the most life-changing decision you have ever made, or will ever make. It will also be the most worthwhile decision you have ever made. Do not let others tell you that you cannot have the life of your dreams. They may tell you that you are living an illusion, but in fact it is they who are deluded. It is your right and your destiny – embrace it.

We each have our lessons to learn and our own paths to tread. If you concentrate on your lessons and your path, you will quickly find yourself living beyond your dreams.

Further reading

Yvonne Aburrow, *Auguries and Omens*
CAPALL BANN PUBLISHING, 1994

Yvonne Aburrow, *The Enchanted Forest*
CAPALL BANN PUBLISHING, 1993

Andy Baggott, *Celtic Wisdom*
PIATKUS BOOKS, 1999

Andy Baggott, *Runes*
ANNESS PUBLISHING, 1999

Ann Faraday, *Dream Power*
PAN BOOKS, 1972

Sigmund Freud, *The Interpretation of Dreams*
PENGUIN BOOKS, 1975

Patricia Garfield, *Dream Messenger*
SIMON AND SCHUSTER, 1997

Nicholas Heyneman, *Dreamscapes: Creating New Realities to Transform and Heal Your Life*
FIRESIDE, 1996

LaBerge and Rheinhold, *Exploring the World of Lucid Dreaming*
BALLANTINE BOOKS, 1991

Susan Lavender and Anna Franklin,
Herb Craft
CAPALL BANN PUBLISHING, 1996

Linda Lane Magallon, *Mutual Dreaming*
POCKET BOOKS, 1997

Stephen Policoff, *Dreamer's Companion*
CHICAGO REVIEW, 1997

Alan Siegel and Kelly Bulkeley,
Dreamcatching: Every Parent's Guide to Understanding and Exploring Children's Dreams and Nightmares
THREE RIVERS PRESS, 1998

Kathleen Sullivan, *Recurring Dreams: A Journey to Wholeness*
CROSSING PRESS, 1998

Jeremy Taylor, *The Living Labyrinth: Exploring Universal Themes in Myths, Dreams, and the Symbolism of Waking Life*
PAULIST PRESS, 1998

Barbara G. Walker, *The Woman's Dictionary of Symbols and Sacred Objects*
HARPERCOLLINS, 1988

Index

Index

Acknowledgments
I would like to thank my partner Debbie for her support and objectivity, Michael Baggott for sharing his dream diary, and Jean Blackaby for her insights. Thanks also to my agent Susan Mears and to all at Godsfield Press for making this part of my dream reality.